SEMA INSTITUTE

P.O.Box 570459
Miami, Florida, 33257
(305) 378-6253 Fax: (305) 378-6253

First U.S. edition © 2006 By Reginald Muata Ashby

All rights reserved. No part of this book may be used or reproduced in any manner whatsoever without written permission (address above) except in the case of brief quotations embodied in critical articles and reviews. All inquiries may be addressed to the address above.

The author is available for group lectures and individual counseling. For further information contact the publisher.

Ashby, Muata
The Black Ancient Egyptians: Evidences of the Black African Origins of Ancient Egyptian Culture, Civilization, Religion and Philosophy
ISBN: 1-884564-21-6 (Softcover)

Library of Congress Cataloging in Publication Data

TABLE OF CONTENTS

Preface: Ethnicity, Race as Culture Factors *4*

Foreword: Introduction to Ancient Egyptian Culture and Civilization *7*
   Where is the land of Egypt? 7

When Was Ancient Egyptian Civilization? *12*
   A Brief History of Ancient Egypt 12

The Controversy Over the "Race" of the Ancient Egyptians (Kamitans) in European Scholarship and the Move to Refute the Testimony of the Seventeenth- and Eighteenth-century European Travelers to Egypt *14*
   References to the Nubian Genealogy of Kamitans in Kamitan Texts and Monuments 23

Color Plates *29*

The Terms Kamit, "Ethiopia," "Nubia," "Kush" and "Sudan" *71*
   The Term Kamit (Qamit, Kamit, Kamit) and Its Relation to Nubia and the term "Black" 71

Ancient Ethiopia (present day Sudan), Called Nubia or Kash by the Ancient Egyptians, As the Source of Great Cultures in Ancient Times *72*
   Colchis, Mesopotamia and Ancient Egypt in the First Millennium B.C.E. 74
   Descriptions of the Nubians (Ethiopians) by the Ancient Greeks 75
   Descriptions of the Ancient Egyptians and Nubians (Ethiopians) by the Ancient Greeks 76
   Evidence of Contact-Eye Witness Accounts, Anthropology, Linguistics, Mythology 77

Assyrian Descriptions of the Ancient Egyptians and Nubians *85*

Ancient Egyptian Depictions of Greek Pharaohs *86*

Ancient Egyptian Depictions of Egyptians (themselves) and Nubians *87*

Images created by early Arab and European Explorers of the Ancient Egyptian Great Sphinx *95*
   Images of People in Ancient Egypt with "African Features" in the Ancient Period and the Late Period of Ancient Egyptian History 98

DNA, Race and Ethnicity *99*

Other Evidences *101*

NOTES and REFERENCES *102*

Index *104*

Other Books From C M Books *108*

Preface: Ethnicity, Race as Culture Factors

This book is a compilation of several sections of a larger work, a book by the name of *African Origins of Civilization, Religion, Yoga Mysticism and Ethics Philosophy*. It is one of several compiled short volumes that has been compiled so as to facilitate access to specific subjects contained in the larger work which is over 680 pages long. These short and small volumes have been specifically designed to cover one subject in a brief and low cost format.

This present volume, *The Black Ancient Egyptians: The Black African Ancestry of the Ancient Egyptians,* formed one subject in the larger work: *The African Origins of Civilization, Religion, Yoga Mysticism and Ethics Philosophy*. It was felt that this subject needed to be discussed because even in the early 21st century, the idea persists that the Ancient Egyptians were peoples originally from Asia Minor who came into North-East Africa. Yet there is ample evidence from ancient writings and perhaps more importantly, iconographical evidences from the Ancient Egyptians themselves that proves otherwise. This handy volume has been designed to be accessible to young adults and all others who would like to have an easy reference with documentation on this important subject. This is an important subject because the frame of reference with which we look at a culture depends strongly on our conceptions about its origins. in this case, if we look at the Ancient Egyptians as Asiatic peoples we would treat them and their culture in one way. If we see them as Africans we not only see them in a different light but we also must ascribe Africa with a glorious legacy that matches any other culture in human history. We would also look at the culture and philosophies of the Ancient Egyptians as having African insights instead of Asiatic ones. Those insights inform our knowledge bout other African traditions and we can also begin to understand in a deeper way the effect of Ancient Egyptian culture on African culture and also on the Asiatic as well.

Modern scientists and scholars say that race distinctions based on genetics is unscientific and wrong. The animosity and hatred of modern times, caused by distortion of religious scriptures when being rewritten or reinterpreted by various groups or ignorance of the true intent of the teachings of the religious holy books, has led to a situation where social problems have rendered practitioners of religion incapable of reaching a higher level of spiritual understanding. Many people in modern society are caught up in the degraded level of disputes and wars in an attempt to support ideas, which are in reality absurd and destructive in reference to the authentic doctrines of religion. Ironically, the inability of leaders in the church, synagogue or secular society to accept the truth about the origins of humanity comes from their desire to gain and maintain control and fear of losing control over their followers. Now that modern science is showing that all human beings originated from the same source, in Africa, and that racial distinctions are at least questionable and misleading and at worst, malicious lies and race baiting, it means that those who have perpetrated and sustained racism can no longer use science or religious teachings to support their iniquity and ignorant designs. They have no leg to stand on. The following excerpt was taken from Encarta Encyclopedia, and is typical of the modern scientific understanding of the question of human genetics and race issues.

> "The concept of race has often been misapplied. One of the most telling arguments against classifying people into races is that persons in various cultures have often mistakenly acted as if one race were superior to another. Although, with social disadvantages eliminated, it is possible that one human group or another might have some genetic advantages in response to such factors as climate, altitude, and specific food availability, these differences are small. There

are no differences in native intelligence or mental capacity that cannot be explained by environmental circumstances. Rather than using racial classifications to study human variability, anthropologists today define geographic or social groups by geographic or social criteria. They then study the nature of the genetic attributes of these groups and seek to understand the causes of changes in their genetic makeup. Contributed by: Gabriel W. Laser "Races, Classification of," Encarta." Copyright (c) 1994

It should be noted here that there is no evidence that racial classifications for the purpose of supporting racist views existed in Ancient Egypt. However, the concept of ethnicity, which is often erroneously confused with the modern concept of race, was acknowledged in ancient times. That is to say, the Ancient Egyptians recognized that some of the physical features and characteristics of the Asiatics, Europeans, and other groups were different from themselves and the Nubians. They recognized themselves as looking like the Nubians, but as possessing differences in culture. The Ancient Egyptian's depictions of themselves and their neighbors show us beyond reasonable doubt, that they were dark skinned people like all other Africans, before the influx of Asiatics and Europeans to the country. Since genetics is increasingly being recognized as a false method of differentiating people the concept of phenotype has progressively more been used.

> **phe·no·type** (fē'nə-tīp') *n.* **1.a.** The observable physical or biochemical characteristics of an organism, as determined by both genetic makeup and environmental influences. **b.** The expression of a specific trait, such as stature or blood type, based on genetic and environmental influences. **2.** An individual or group of organisms exhibiting a particular phenotype.[i]

It has been shown that climactic conditions, geography, solar exposure, vegetation, etc., have the effect of changing the appearance of people. This means that while people (human beings) remain equally human internally, their physiognomy and shade of skin adapt to the conditions where they live. This means that the external differences in people have little to do with their internal humanity and therefore are illusory. The concept of social typing is therefore based on ignorance about the race issue and its misconceptions, and cannot be supported by the scientific evidences. Further, an advancing society cannot hold such erroneous notions without engendering strife, and confusion, within the society. An advancing society will not be able to attain the status of "civilization" while holding on to such spurious concepts.

One of the major problems for society and non-secular groups is that the teachings and scientific evidence presented here has not been taught to the world population at large as part of the public or private education system. Even if it were, it would take time for people to adjust to their new understanding. Most people grow up accepting the ignorance of their parents who received the erroneous information from their own parents, and so on. Racism, sexism and other scourges of society are not genetically transmitted. They are transmitted by ignorant family members who pass on their ignorance, prejudices and bigotries to their children, and so on down through the generations.

The only fair and accurate standard to classify people is by means of education and ethics. Here education refers not just to trades or technical endeavors but to the origins of humanity and the contributions of all members (especially the Africans) of humanity to the evolution of world culture and the advancement towards civilization. This knowledge directly impacts a person's

---

[i] American Heritage Dictionary

ethics, as once the common origins of humanity and the falseness of the race issue are understood and affirmed in a person's life, their ethics, and relations this will have an impact on how people view each other and consequently this will improve how people treat each other.

Black, White and In-between.

The use of the words "Black", "White" to describe people is not to be taken as a racial description. According to the ancient wisdom as well as modern genetics, there is only one race, the human race. The use of these words in this volume is only applied in order to relate to terms that are commonly used, for lack of a better language in the public sector. Nevertheless it is used here to turn around the misuse they have suffered in many literatures from racist societies. Therefore, the reader should keep in mind that the use of these terms is for descriptive purposes, as features of ethnic groups, and not as racial groups.

Foreword: Introduction to Ancient Egyptian Culture and Civilization

Where is the land of Egypt?

A map of North East Africa showing the location of the land of *Ta-Meri* or *Kamut,* also known as Ancient Egypt:

The Ancient Egyptians lived for thousands of years in the northeastern corner of the African continent in the area known as the Nile Valley. The Nile River was a source of dependable enrichment for the land and allowed them to prosper for a very long time. Their prosperity was so great that they created art, culture, religion, philosophy and a civilization which has not been duplicated ever since. The Ancient Kamitans (Egyptians) based their government and business concerns on spiritual values and therefore, enjoyed an orderly society which included equality between the sexes, and a legal system based on universal spiritual laws. The *Egyptian Mystery System* is a tribute to their history, culture and legacy. As historical insights unfold, it becomes clearer that modern culture has derived its basis from Ancient Egypt, though the credit is not often given, nor the integrity of the practices maintained in the new religions. This is another important reason to study Ancient Egyptian Philosophy, to discover the principles which allowed their civilization to prosper over a period of thousands of years in order to bring our systems of government, religion and social structures to a harmony with ourselves, humanity and with nature.

The flow of the Nile brought annual floods to the Nile Valley and this provided irrigation and new soil nutrients every year that allowed for regular crops when worked on time. This regularity and balance of nature inspired the population to adopt a culture of order and duty based on cosmic order: Maat. This idea extends to the understanding of Divine justice and reciprocity. So if work is performed on time and in cooperation with nature, there will be order, balance and peace as well as prosperity in life.

Kamit (Egypt) is located in the north-eastern corner of the continent of Africa. It is composed of towns along the banks of the Hapi (Nile River). In the north there is the Nile Delta region where the river contacts the Mediterranean Sea. This part is referred to as the North or Lower Egypt, "lower," because that is the lowest elevation and the river flows from south to north. The middle of the country is referred to as Middle Egypt. The south is referred to as Upper Egypt because it is the higher elevation and the river flows from there to the north. The south is the older region of the dynastic civilization and the middle and north are later.

The Black African Ancient Egyptians

From Ancient times Egypt was regarded by the Ancient Egyptians as being composed of three regions: Upper Egypt (south), Middle Egypt (middle), and Lower Egypt (north).

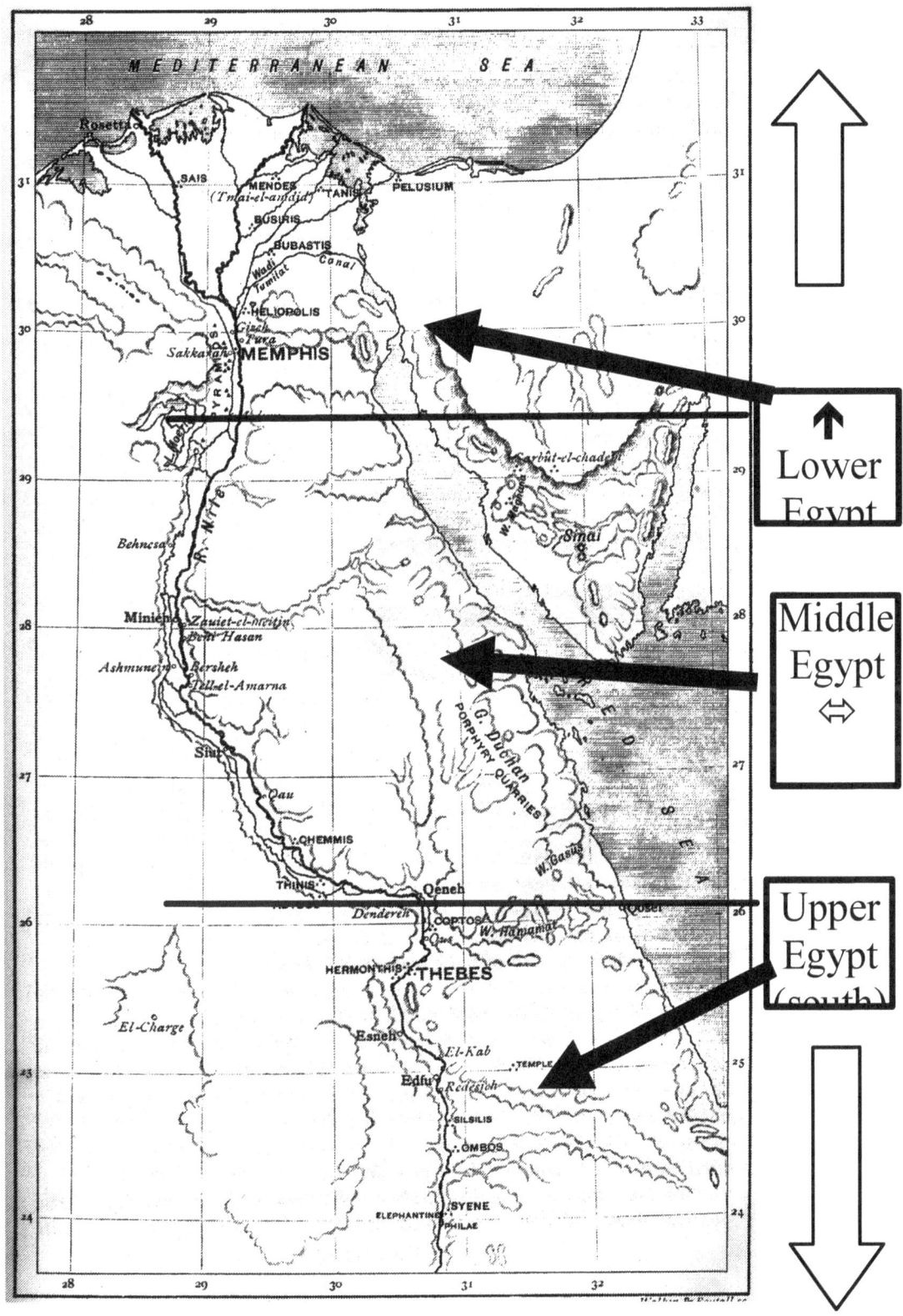

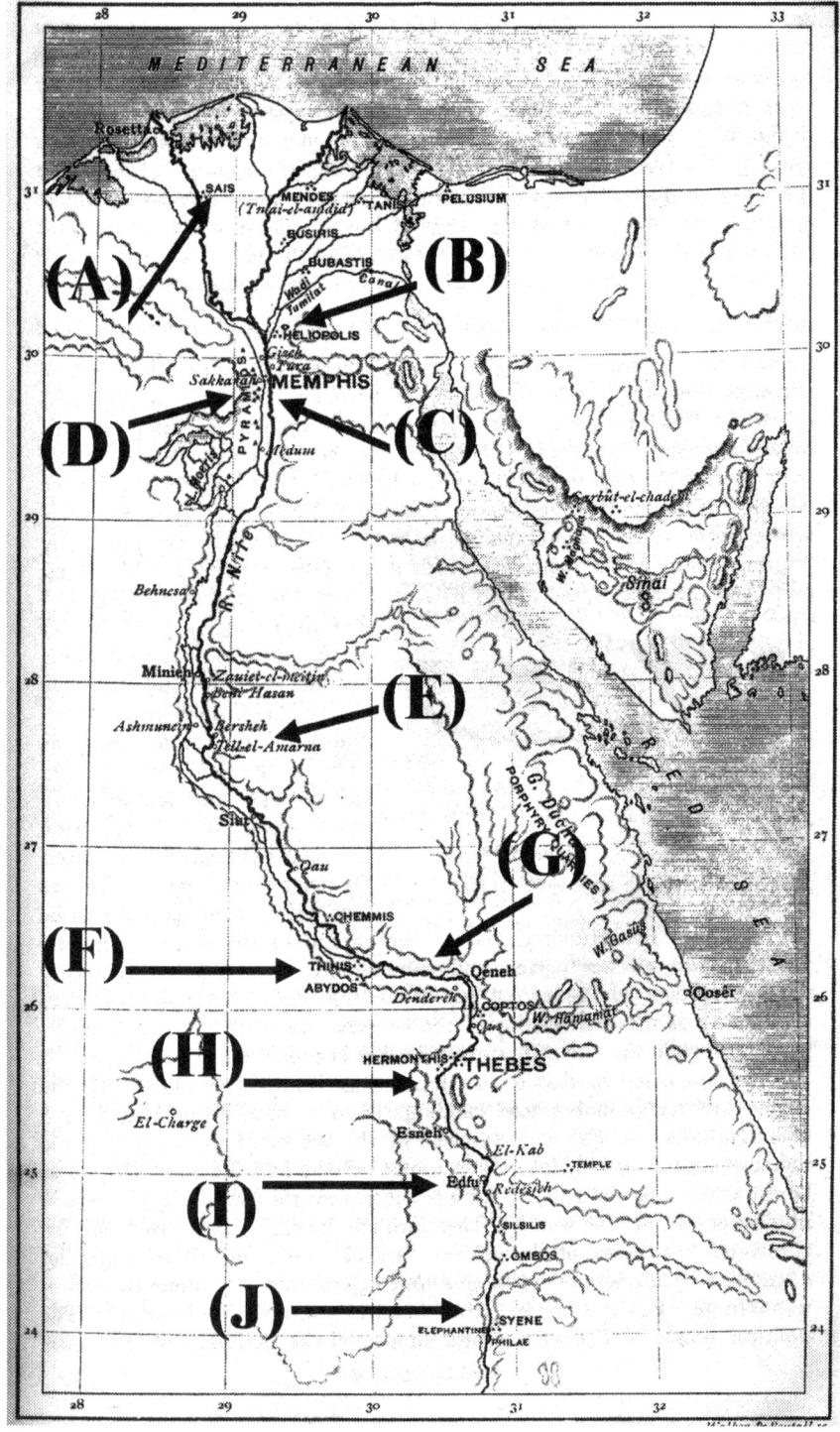

Left- The Ancient Egyptian cities were related to certain divinities and their respective religious theologies. The Land of Ancient Egypt-Nile Valley - The cities wherein the theology of the Trinity of Amun-Ra-Ptah was developed were: A- Sais (temple of Net), B- Anu (Heliopolis- temple of Ra), C- Men-nefer or Hetkaptah (Memphis, temple of Ptah), and D- Sakkara (Pyramid Texts), E- Akhet-Aton (City of Akhnaton, temple of Aton), F- Abdu (temple of Asar)-Greek Abydos, G- Denderah (temple of Hetheru), H- Waset (Thebes, temple of Amun), I- Edfu (temple of Heru), J- Philae (temple of Aset). The cities wherein the theology of the Trinity of Asar-Aset-Heru was developed were Anu, Abdu, Philae, Denderah and Edfu.

The Sphinx and its contemporary architecture throughout Kamit give us the earliest history, the earliest recorded evidence of the practice of advanced religion anywhere in the world. The Sphinx has now been proven to be the earliest example of the practice of religion in human history, 10,000 BCE.

The next religion appears in India at about 2,500 to 3,000 BCE. We have shown in the book *African Origins* that there was a direct relationship between the Indians and the Ancient Egyptians/Ancient Africans, so much so that the basic tenants of Hinduism and Buddhism can be directly correlated to Shetaut Neter.

Before the Songai Empire
　Before Timbuktu
　　Before the Mali Empire
　　Before the Ghana Empire
　　Before Islam
　　　Before Christianity
　　　Before the Sumerians
　　　　Before the Greek Civilization
　　　Before the Roman Empire
　　Before Hinduism
　　　Before Buddhism
　　Before Europe
　　　Before The United States

THERE WAS

KAMIT

When Was Ancient Egyptian Civilization?

A Brief History of Ancient Egypt

Christianity was partly an outgrowth of Judaism, which was itself an outgrowth of Ancient Egyptian culture and religion. So who were the Ancient Egyptians? From the time that the early Greek philosophers set foot on African soil to study the teachings of mystical spirituality in Egypt (900-300 B.C.E.), Western society and culture was forever changed. Ancient Egypt had such a profound effect on Western civilization as well as on the native population of Ancient India (Dravidians) that it is important to understand the history and culture of Ancient Egypt, and the nature of its spiritual tradition in more detail.

The history of Egypt begins in the far reaches of history. It includes The Dynastic Period, The Hellenistic Period, Roman and Byzantine Rule (30 B.C.E.-638 A.C.E.), the Caliphate and the Mamalukes (642-1517 A.C.E.), Ottoman Domination (1082-1882 A.C.E.), British colonialism (1882-1952 A.C.E.), as well as modern, Arab-Islamic Egypt (1952- present).

Ancient Egypt or Kamit, was a civilization that flourished in Northeast Africa along the Nile River from before 5,500 B.C.E. until 30 B.C.E. In 30 B.C.E., Octavian, who was later known as the Roman Emperor, Augustus, put the last Egyptian King, Ptolemy XIV, a Greek ruler, to death. After this Egypt was formally annexed to Rome. Egyptologists normally divide Ancient Egyptian history into the following periods: The Early Dynastic Period; The Old Kingdom or Old Empire; The First Intermediate Period; The Middle Kingdom or Middle Empire; The Second Intermediate Period; The New Kingdom or New Empire (1,532-1,070 B.C.E.); The third Intermediate Period (1,070-712 B.C.E.); The Late Period (712-332 B.C.E.).

In the Late Period the following groups controlled Egypt. The Nubian Dynasty (712-657 B.C.E.); The Persian Dynasty (525-404 B.C.E.); The Native Revolt and re-establishment of Egyptian rule by Egyptians (404-343 B.C.E.); The Second Persian Period (343-332 B.C.E.); The Ptolemaic or Greek Period (332 B.C.E.- c. 30 B.C.E.); Roman Period (c.30 B.C.E.-395 A.C.E.); The Byzantine Period (395-640 A.C.E) and The Arab Conquest Period (640 A.C.E.-present). The individual dynasties are numbered, generally in Roman numerals, from I through XXX. However, the realization of the geological evidence of the Great Sphinx and the discovery of the new Dynasty previously unknown to the Egyptologists, the history needs to be revised. See the full revision in the book *African Origins of Civilization* by Muata Ashby (2002).

The period after the New Kingdom saw greatness in culture and architecture under the rulership of Ramses II. However, after his rule, Egypt saw a decline from which it would never recover. This is the period of the downfall of Ancient Egyptian culture in which the Libyans ruled after the Tanite (XXI) Dynasty. This was followed by the Nubian conquerors who founded the XXII Dynasty and tried to restore Egypt to her past glory. However, having been weakened by the social and political turmoil of wars, Ancient Egypt fell to the Persians once more. The Persians conquered the country until the Greeks, under Alexander, conquered them. The Romans followed the Greeks, and finally the Arabs conquered the land of Egypt in 640 A.C.E to the present.

However, the history which has been classified above is only the history of the "Dynastic Period." It reflects the view of traditional Egyptologists who have refused to accept the evidence of a Predynastic period in Ancient Egyptian history contained in Ancient Egyptian documents such as the *Palermo Stone, Royal Tablets at Abydos, Royal Papyrus of Turin,* the *Dynastic List* of *Manetho,* and the eye-witness accounts of Greek historians Herodotus (c. 484-425 B.C.E.) and

Diodorus. These sources speak clearly of a Pre-dynastic society which stretches far into antiquity. The Dynastic Period is what most people think of whenever Ancient Egypt is mentioned. This period is when the pharaohs (kings) ruled. The latter part of the Dynastic Period is when the Biblical story of Moses, Joseph, Abraham, etc., occurs (c. 2100? -1,000? B.C.E). Therefore, those with a Christian background generally only have an idea about Ancient Egypt as it is related in the Bible. The tradition based on the old Jewish bible recounting about how the Jews were used for forced labor and the construction of the great monuments of Egypt such as the Great Pyramids is impossible since these were created in the predynastic age, thousands of years before Abraham, the supposed first Jew, ever existed. Although this biblical notion is very limited in scope, the significant impact of Ancient Egypt on Hebrew and Christian culture is evident even from the biblical scriptures. Actually, Egypt existed much earlier than most traditional Egyptologists are prepared to admit. The new archeological evidence related to the great Sphinx monument on the Giza Plateau and the ancient writings by Manetho, one of the last High Priests of Ancient Egypt, show that Ancient Egyptian history begins earlier than 10,000 B.C.E. and may date back to as early as 30,000-50,000 B.C.E.

The Controversy Over the "Race" of the Ancient Egyptians (Kamitans) in European Scholarship and the Move to Refute the Testimony of the Seventeenth- and Eighteenth-century European Travelers to Egypt

The move to deny the appearance of the Ancient Egyptians and promote the idea that they were not African at all has been put forth by many western writers, even in the face of the writings of the Ancient Egyptians themselves who attest:

1. They are ancestors of the Nubians, to the south, in Africa.
2. Their own depictions of themselves as dark or "black" skinned people.
3. The descriptions of them as "black" people, by the Greek classical writers.
4. The genealogies provided by the Ancient Egyptians themselves stating that their parents are Nubian (such as Amunmhat I).

Jean Fransçois Champollion (1790 A.C.E.-1832 A.C.E.), the main decipherer of the hieroglyphic text in the early 19th century, who is often referred to as the "Father of Egyptology", remarked at the art he saw, which at the time was fully colored since the tombs and many other structures had been closed since the Middle Ages (Dark Ages). He described images of the Ancient Egyptians, created by them, in which they made themselves look like the Ethiopians, and concluded that they were of the same "race" as the modern day Nubians, who are "black" skinned African peoples, saying in a letter to his brother that he wrote while in Egypt examining the reliefs and studying the hieroglyphs: *"We find there Egyptians and Africans represented in the same way"*.[1] Jean Fransçois Champollion later states that based on the images he saw it was clear that the Ancient Egyptians looked like the people presently living in Nubia, i.e. they were "black Africans."

In this same manner, Count Volney wrote after a trip to Egypt between 1783 and 1785:

> "Just think that this race of black men, today our slave and the object of our scorn, is the very race to which we owe our arts, sciences and even the use of speech! Just imagine, finally, that it is in the midst of people who call themselves the greatest friends of liberty and humanity that one has approved the most barbarous slavery and questioned whether black men have the same kind of intelligence as whites!"[2]

Some of the travelers and explorers of the 19th century were *Livingstone, Speke, Baker and Junker*. Documenting the observations of travelers such as Livingstone, and others J. A Rogers recorded the following statements by them in his book *Sex and Race Vol. I*:

> "Livingstone said that the Negro face as he saw it reminded him more of that on the monuments of ancient Assyria than that of the popular white fancy.[3] Sir Harry Johnston, foremost authority on the African Negro, said that "the Hamite," that Negroid stock which was the main stock of the ancient Egyptians, is best represented at the present day by the Somali, Galla, and the blood of Abyssinia and Nubia."[4] Sergi compares pictorially the features of Ramases II with that of Mtesa, noted Negro king of Uganda, and show the marked resemblance.[5] Sir M. W. Flinders Petrie, famed Egyptologist says that the Pharaohs of the Xth dynasty were of the Galla type, and the Gallas are clearly what are known in our day as Negroes. He tells further of seeing one day on a train a man whose features were "the exact living, type" of a statue of ancient Libya, and discovered that the man was a American mulatto.[6]"

The stir that the early descriptions of the Egyptians based on their own depictions, as described and reproduced by early explorers and artists, created in Europe in the early years of Egyptology after the translation of the hieroglyphic language by Champollion (1822 A.C.E.) was an unforeseen controversy that later Egyptologists tried desperately to refute. The following memoir recorded by Champollion-Figeac, the brother of Jean Fransçois Champollion in 1829 denotes the "problem," which the western researchers who recognized the importance of Ancient Egyptian civilization, were facing. It was obvious that the writings were beginning to reveal religion, philosophy and evolved culture, all of which contradict the basic tenets used to justify the denigration of the "Negro" race and their enslavement in Africa, Europe and the "New World" (the Americas). Therefore, it became necessary to refute and even attempt to explain away the reason for the findings. (underlined portions by Ashby)

> The opinion that the ancient population of Egypt belonged to the Negro African race, is an error long accepted as the truth. Since the Renaissance, travelers in the East, barely capable of fully appreciating the ideas provided by Egyptian monuments on this important question, have helped to spread that false notion and geographers have not failed to reproduce it, even in our day. A serious authority declared himself in favor of this view and popularized the error. Such was the effect of what the celebrated Volney published on the various races of men that he had observed in Egypt. In his *Voyage,* which is in all libraries, he reports that the Copts are descended from the ancient Egyptians; that <u>the Copts have a bloated face, puffed up eyes, flat nose, and thick lips, like a mulatto; that they resemble the Sphinx of the Pyramids, a distinctly Negro head</u>. He concludes that the ancient Egyptians were true Negroes of the same species as all indigenous Africans. To support his opinion, Volney invokes that of Herodotus who, apropos the Colchians, recalls that the <u>Egyptians had black skin and woolly hair.</u> <u>Yet these two physical qualities do not suffice to characterize the Negro race</u> and Volney's conclusion as to the Negro origin of the ancient Egyptian civilization is evidently forced and inadmissible.
>
> It is recognized today that the inhabitants of Africa belong to three races, quite distinct from each other for all time: 1. Negroes proper, in Central and West Africa; 2. Kaffirs on the east coast, who have a less obtuse facial angle than

Blacks and a high nose, but thick lips and woolly hair; 3. Moors, similar in stature, physiognomy and hair to the *best-formed* nations of Europe and western Asia, and differing only in skin color which is tanned by the climate. The ancient population of Egypt belonged to this latter race, that is, to the white race. To be convinced of this, we need only examine the human figures representing Egyptians on the monuments and above all the great number of mummies that have been opened. Except for the color of the skin, blackened by the hot climate, they are the same men as those of Europe and western Asia: frizzy, woolly hair is the true characteristic of the Negro race; the Egyptians, however, had long hair, identical with that of the white race of the West.[7]

Firstly, Champollion-Figeac affirms that the ancient "Egyptians had black skin and woolly hair." However, he and then goes on to say that these are not sufficient to characterize the Negro race. He thus contradicts himself later by saying "frizzy, woolly hair is the true characteristic of the Negro race." Obviously this is a contradiction in terms that is inescapable. In an attempt to formulate a thesis that the Ancient Egyptians were essentially "white people," like "the best-formed" Europeans, "except for the color of the skin, blackened by the hot climate," he stumbles on his own argument which is unreasonable at the outset. At no time previous or since has there been recognized anywhere on earth, a "race" of white-black people. This argument is based on observing the so-called "three races" of Africa of his time, as if these were representative of the ancient ethnicity of Africa and could have any baring on the question of the "race" of the Ancient Egyptians. This argument is of course contradictory and unworkable such as it is, but even more so when it is kept in mind that the Ancient Egyptians mixed with Asiatics and Europeans (Greeks) and even still the descriptions of the classical Greek writers unanimously considered them as what in the present day would be called "Negros." Also, the present day Copts, descendants of the Ancient Egyptians, of Champollion-Figeac's time were even then recognized as having "Negroid" features. By Champollion-Figeac's reasoning it would be necessary to conclude that Africans are white Europeans. The Kaffirs (Muslim word for pagans) being referred to are those people whom the Muslim Arabs found in Africa as they entered Africa from the Sinai Peninsula, which is the bridge between Asia Minor and Africa. From there they captured the countries in North Africa from Egypt, to Libya, Tunisia, Algiers and Morocco as well as Spain. Through limited genealogies left by the Moors it has been determined that they were a mixture of Arab and African blood.

Thus, the comparisons used by Champollion-Figeac are wholly useless for determining the "race" of the Ancient Egyptians, but they can however be used for comparisons to the Copts, who like the Moors, appeared to "have a bloated face, puffed up eyes, flat nose, and thick lips, like a mulatto" like the Moors, and also like the present day peoples of African descent living in the Diaspora (African Americans, African Brazilians, Africans in Jamaica, etc.). When this kind of comparison is made it is clear that the "mulatto" arises from a combination of African and Semite (Arab) or European. This of course means that the African features, (color of the skin, thick lips and woolly hair) must have been present in the past if they are present in the current population of mixed peoples, that is to say, the population goes from "black" skin to "lighter" skin color and not the other way around. Except for the effects of climactic changes on populations over a long period of time (thousands of years), which have been shown to cause changes in physical appearance, there is no record of "Black" populations arising from "white" populations. Lastly, in the time of the Ancient Egyptians, before the coming of the Greeks, there were no Europeans in Africa at all. The only populations recognized by the Egyptians were themselves, the other Africans, the Libyans and the Asiatics, all of whom vary in skin tone from dark "black" to light "brown" coloration. So if there are any "white" people in present day Africa they are descendants of the documented influx of Greeks who came in as invading forces with Alexander the Great (330 B.C.E.) and or the documented influx of Arabs which came with the advent of the expansion of Islam (650 B.C.E.) and after. In any case, when discussing the Ancient Egyptians of the Old and Middle Kingdoms and the Pre-Dynastic Period, we are not discussing "mulattos" since the admixture with other ethnic groups had not occurred until the New Kingdom period, and even more so in the Late period, through contact with the conquering Asiatic and European forces. Therefore, to look at the images of the Egyptians during the mixture period and to say that these are representative of the Ancient Egyptian ethnic origins is the worst kind of scholarship. This is a tactic used by some Western and Arab scholars to escape the conclusion that the Ancient Egyptians were "black." How is this possible? In places such as the United States of America, the "rule" established by the "white" ruling class has always been that "one drop of black blood make one black." This means that everyone from dark black skin color to the light brown or swarthy complexion, are recognized as being descendants of the African slaves, and are subject to being segregated and discriminated against. But in this argument it is also possible to say that those mulattos are not 100% African since they are mixed with European, Arab, etc. So they are trying to say that the Ancient Egyptians were either a mixed race or better yet, an indigenous Asiatic group that developed independently of the "black Africans." In any case, even in the late period the Greek classical writers witnessed the population of Kamit as being overwhelmingly "black" (Nubian). So we are not talking about "light skinned black people" or "dark skinned white people" but "dark skinned black people," like those who can be met even today (2002 A.C.E.) in the city of Aswan (Upper (southern) Egypt – see picture above).

There were several prominent and respected Linguists and Egyptologists who affirmed that the Ancient Egyptians were "African" or "Negros." Sir Henry Rawlinson, prominent linguist and decipherer of the mideastern scripts and widely regarded as the "father of Middle-Eastern Studies," said *"Seti's face is thoroughly African, strong, fierce, prognathous, with depressed nose, thick lips and a heavy chin..."*[8] Showing that certain foremost Egyptologists accept the "Negro" composition of the Ancient Egyptian people, J. A Rogers recorded the following statements by the famous British Egyptologist Flinders Petrie, in his book *Sex and Race Vol.I*:

> "Egyptian civilization, from its beginning to the Christian era, lasted for more than seven thousand years, that is, about four times as long as from "the birth of Christ" to the present, therefore, most of the records have been lost, and the little that remains must be pieced together. There are often great gaps. Between the Bushman period of 9000 B.C. and the First Dynasty (4477-4514 B.C.) very little is known. Some of the faces of the rulers of this dynasty are clearly Negroid. The founder of the Third Dynasty, Sa-nekht, was a full-blooded Negro, a type commonly seen in the Egyptian army today. Petrie says of him, "It will be seen how strongly Ethiopian the characters of it (the portrait) is even more so than Shabaka, most marked of the Ethiopian dynasty. The type is one with which we are very familiar among the Sudanese of the Egyptian police and army; it goes with a dark-brown skin and a very truculent character."

In the late 19th century (A.C.E.) the French director general of the Egyptian Service of Antiquities and regarded as a foremost Egyptologist, Gaston Maspero (1846-1916 A.C.E.), wrote about the controversy about the origins and descriptions of the Ancient Egyptians as it stood in his times. (underlined portions by Ashby)

"In our day the origin and ethnographic affinities of the population <u>have inspired lengthy debate</u>. First, the seventeenth- and eighteenth-century travelers, <u>misled by the appearance of certain mongrelized Copts</u>, certified that their predecessors in the Pharaonic age had a <u>puffed up face, bug eyes, flat nose, fleshy lips</u>. And that they presented certain <u>characteristic features of the Negro race</u>. This error, common at the start of the century, vanished once and for all as soon as the French Commission had published its great work."[9]

One of the questions that arise here is why was the unanimous reaction of the seventeenth- and eighteenth-century European travelers in Egypt so upsetting to the late eighteenth and twentieth century western scholars? They were the first Europeans in modern times to see the Ancient Egyptian reliefs and paintings and their reaction was the same as the Greek classical writers when it came to describing the peoples of Kamit and the rest of the Nile Valley. In fact, they did not base their assessment of the Ancient Egyptian ethnicity just by examining their descendants, the Copts, but on images left behind by the Kamitans, some that had been buried under the encroaching dessert sands, which for this reasons were preserved in very good condition. It is interesting to note that the appearance of the Copts was acknowledged as presenting the "mongrelized" features (<u>puffed up face, bug eyes, flat nose, fleshy lips</u>) and that these are understood as being generally representative of the "Negro race." This observation has been widely accepted by all who agree with the concept of ethnic differentiations among human populations. Yet, when it comes to acknowledging these features in the images of Ancient Egypt they become somehow unrepresentative or unreliable or insufficient in assisting in the determination about where those people came from and to which population they are related.

This move to obfuscate the issue gained momentum in the 20th century and became widely accepted by society in general, despite all the evidence to the contrary. Even in the late 20th century there are anthropologists and Egyptologists staunchly supporting the baseless construct of an other than "Negro" origin of the Ancient Egyptians. What has changed is the willingness to say that they were Africans. What has not changed is the reluctance to accept their "blackness." Being unable to refute the pictorial evidences or the writings by the Egyptians themselves, many present day researches who seek to prove that the Ancient Egyptians were not "black" Africans attempt to use other means to discredit the findings which do not support their contentions.

The work of a western scholar by the name of Martin Bernal, author of *Black Athena : The Afroasiatic Roots of Classical Civilization (The Fabrication of Ancient Greece 1785-1985*, (published in 1989), a scathing report on the western falsification of the evidences pointing to an African origin of Greek (i.e. Western civilization) received a storm of criticism from some researchers who propose that his treatment of the statements by the classical Greek writers as "eager credulity." Jacques Berlinerblan, the author of *Heresy in the University: The Black Athena Controversy and the Responsibilities of American Intellectuals* (1999) examines the charge against Bernal.

"With this generous reading now rendered I would like to note that Bernal has offered no viable alternative or corrective to the approaches which he believes are responsible for the fall of the Ancient Model. Nor does he distinguish among better or worse types of exegetical and hermeneutic approaches, leaving us with the impression that he believes all are equally corrupt. His methodological credo seems to be *The Ancients could very well be telling us the truth*. While this is plausible, it is incumbent upon the author to advance a method which might help us to determine how scholars might go about distinguishing truthful accounts from untruthful ones. As Egyptologist John D. Ray asked, "Where are the final criteria to lie?" To this point, Bernal has neglected to articulate such criteria, and this leaves him vulnerable to Mary Lefkowitz's charge of "eager credulity" toward the ancient sources."[10]

There is an interesting process of selective acceptance of certain evidences from the ancient writers and overlooking or minimizing certain other evidences when it is convenient to explain a particular point. This is noticeable in the work of some western scholars of Ancient Egypt, Greece as well as India. Bernal's book drew such criticism, not because the information was new, since other writers such as Cheikh Anta Diop had presented it in his book *African Origins of Civilization, Myth or Reality*. The problem was that Bernal is a "white" European scholar, part of the establishment, and the information he presented was perceived by some of his peers as precipitating the fall of the walls of western academia's characterization of African civilization, and consequently the history of western civilization, and their prestige as western scholars with it. The objective here also seems to call into question the veracity of the ancient writers, or to say that they were gullible, or to make it appear that their Egyptian "guides" or "informants" were trying to impress the Greeks by telling them wild stories that they wanted to hear. In the third chapter of *Not Out of Africa: How Afrocentrism Became an Excuse to Teach Myth As History* (August 1997), Mary Lefkowitz reviews the texts which Bernal used in order to build his Ancient and Revised Ancient Models. "The idea that Greek religion and philosophy has Egyptian origins," she asserts, "may appear at first sight to be more plausible, because it derives, at least in part, from the writings of ancient Greek historians." The scholar Jacques Berlinerblan explains Lefkowitz's position, which he himself admittedly shares. (Underlined portions by Ashby)

> "Lefkowitz advances an unyieldingly critical appraisal of the writings of Herodotus, Diodorus, Plato, Strabo, and the Church Fathers on the subject of Egypt. These figures cannot be counted on to offer us objective accounts due to their "respect for the antiquity of Egyptian religion and civilization, and a desire somehow to be connected with it." This admiration inclined them to overemphasize their dependency on, and contacts with, the land of the Pyramids. But the presence of a pro-Egyptian bias in Greek thought is not the only drawback which Lefkowitz discovers. In true Hard Modern fashion she enumerates the failings of the ancients qua historical researchers. The Greeks were not sufficiently skeptical or critical of their informants and sources. They did not speak Egyptian, nor did they draw upon Egyptian archives. They misunderstood the very Egyptian phenomena they studied. Their linguistic surmises were predicated on simplistic and erroneous assumptions. They looked at Egypt "through cultural blinkers," producing an image that was "astigmatic and deeply Hellenized."[11] Again and again Lefkowitz pounds the point home-how poorly the Greeks performed when compared to us:
> Unlike modern anthropologists, who approach new cultures so far as possible with an open mind, and with the aid of a developed set of methodologies, Herodotus tended to construe whatever he saw by analogy with Greek practice, as if it were impossible for him to comprehend it any other way.
> Lest there exist any remaining question as to the reliability of the ancients, Lefkowitz proceeds to pulverize the final link in the chain of historical

transmission. Not only were <u>the Greeks unreliable, but so were their Egyptian informants</u>. <u>Jewish and Christian Egyptians supplied the gullible Greeks with self-aggrandizing information</u> as "a way of asserting the importance of their culture, especially in a time when they had little or no political powers."[12]

We must keep in mind that scholars such as Lefkowitz are trying to discredit the ancient authors but the arguments of such scholars are not based on rationality or on evidences to prove their contentions.

1. People from different periods in time, removed in some cased by several hundreds of years, which means that they did not have an opportunity to conspire with each other to fabricate the same "fantasies".
2. They did not speak to the same people upon visiting Egypt or in such cases as Pythagoras and Plato, becoming students of the Egyptian masters for several years.
3. They had no reason to lie about their experiences as do present day western scholars, who need to uphold a view of the past that support western superiority and independence from the very people whose oppression is rationalized by saying that they had no culture, religion, philosophy or civilization.
4. The Greek classical writers (Herodotus, Plutarch, Pythagoras, Plato, Aristotle, Diodorus, Strabo, and others) did not rely simply on what they were told by their "informants." They presented evidences and described what they saw with their own eyes and when these descriptions are compared they are in agreement with their statements and with the evidences that can be examined by any person who takes the time to visit a serious museum of Egyptian antiquities or the monuments and tombs of Ancient Egypt themselves.
5. The use of the term "informants" in itself reveals the demeaning attitude and prejudicial manner of dealing with the Greek Classical writers, presumably because there is no other area that these scholars can attack in order to prove their theory.
6. There are ample forms of evidence besides the writings of the Greek classical authors upon which to investigate the ethnicity of the Ancient Egyptians and their contributions to early Greek culture. These other evidences, such as the adoption of Ancient Egyptian customs, tradition and religion by the Greeks are irrefutable and inescapable and therefore, not to be mentioned. By creating a stir in one area, the western researchers hope to cloud the issue and taint an objective observer's view of other evidences.

In any case, such attacks can be easily dismissed since they are entirely without basis. The problem arises in the fact that they speak from a self-serving pulpit, the "western scholarly establishment" that is supported by the western media, which accepts documentaries that are made for television by these scholars or approved by the "legitimate" schools that they represent, rather than from conclusive evidence. Anyone who has worked in the western university setting knows that there is a lot of politics involved with attaining the coveted status as tenured professor. Of course, anyone who does not agree with the established opinions will have a difficult time breaking through the invisible walls of the western "ivory towers." The Western academia, which controls the scholars through the process of selectively accepting those who support the pre-established doctrines and rejecting those who do not. Scholarly criticism is one thing, but dismissing something just because it does not agree with one's views is simply unscientific and evidence of an ulterior motive or hidden agenda. Having the most powerful voice to speak with and being supported by the government, the western scholarly establishment has the capacity to put out skewed images of reality, that when repeated again and again over a period of time, attains a status of being "truth" and "real," but when examined closely, are found to be nothing more that the cries of unhappy children who cannot accept the evidences before them. A fault that was noted in Lefkowitz's work not by the Africentrists or by Bernal but by her own colleague Jacques Berlinerblan, which reveals her duplicitous manner of handling the statements of the Greek classical writers.

> In my own work on the Hebrew Bible I have argued, with no less passion, that we simply cannot believe what this text reports. Accordingly, I concur with her objections, and I find Lefkowitz's overarching skepticism justified. Yet in her haste to skewer Bernal, Lefkowitz avoids considering the drawbacks or implications of her - I should say "our"-position. At one point in Not Out of Africa she speaks of the "important," "generally accurate," and "useful information" which Herodotus makes apropos of the Nile, Egyptian monuments, and individual pharaohs. The problem is that Lefkowitz never pauses to tell us why she considers these particular observations to be "generally accurate." Further, she and other critics of Bernal often evince their own "eager credulity" toward ancient texts, especially when it permits them to criticize Bernal. Lefkowitz, for instance, is not averse to citing and accepting Herodotus's testimony if it helps her to refute *Black Athena's* historical claims.[13]

Lefkowitz's double standard sabotages her own integrity and thus invalidates her statements and motives as a scholar. When the empty attempts to impugn the statements of the Greek classical writers fails there is no recourse but to engage in attempts to discredit the scholars who advance their positions using the "unacceptable" evidences by referring to them as "wild," "flaky," etc., and refer to their positions as based on "fantasies." A western writer by the name of Steven Howe characterized the work of noted Africentric scholars in this way in his book. Without providing any evidence to refute their positions, a practice that is widely regarded as the hallmark of the western scientific process, he presented the opinions of other scholars who agree with him, they also being devoid of evidences to back up their positions. This of course is no scholarship at all, but merely the addition of one more voice to the cacophony of western scholarly discontent over the undeniable and overwhelming evidences contradicting their positions. The absence of real evidence to support their opinions is substituted with forceful opinions and emotional appeals and these cannot be accepted as science, but as disgruntled and frustrated outbursts. Mr. Howe makes the following assertions without supporting these with any evidence either in Egyptology, anthropology, genetics, geology or any other recognized science.

1. The ancient Egyptians belonged to no race, they were neither black nor white but Egyptian.
2. The white race did not evolve from the black.
3. The race concept did not exist in Ancient Egypt.
4. Arabs did not overrun or destroy north Africa.

The obvious misconceptions or misinformation or errors in Mr. Howe's arguments can be easily and concisely proven to be false, since there is no real evidence being presented:

> A. The first point is bogus on its face. Even in the present day, the spurious concept of "racism" recognizes no such race as "Egyptian." All human beings have been regarded by the western race concept as either "white," meaning European, or of

some "Negroid" stock, meaning descendant or affiliated with African ancestry, or fitting into some range of color between "black" and "white."
- B. All the evidences from anthropology and genetic sciences point to a common origin for all modern human beings as having originated in Africa. Therefore, Mr. Howe is either misinformed or deliberately misdirecting the public. Inherent in the treatment of Egyptology is the practice of ignoring the findings of scientific disciplines which are widely regarded as being empirical as opposed to theoretical. These are ignored because they contradict the orthodox dogmatic position. These other sciences support the "black" African origins of Ancient Egyptian culture.
    - i. Mr. Howe proposes the idea that the Ancient Egyptians did not indeed have a concept of race in order to support the idea that there was no difference between how they saw themselves and the other peoples of the world. The Ancient Egyptians were not racists and consequently no record of race classifications, or practices such as those of modern Western Culture have been discovered even after 200 years of Egyptological research. However, the concept of ethnic differentiation did exist. The Ancient Egyptians did recognize and acknowledge the concept of ethnicity which includes an awareness of the differences in physical features like skin color, etc. Several examples of these "ethnographies" survive to this day. So the Ancient Egyptians saw themselves as being the same in appearance to the Nubians and other Africans and different from the Asiatics and the later Greeks (Europeans). Thus, the Greeks (Europeans) could not be Egyptians since the Egyptians depicted themselves as "black" Africans. It is interesting that some scholars try to hold on to the idea that race is not important based on the genetic evidence which shows the race concept to be bogus, when it suits the ideal of asserting that the Egyptians had no race so as not to be forced to admit that they were "black Africans," but when it comes to accepting people of non-European descent into European countries, equality in economics, social settings and government, the practice of segregation and discrimination based on racial bias, remains enforced.
- C. Ample records and evidences from African peoples as well as the Assyrian, Persian, Greek and Arab conquerors attest to the fact of the movement from Europe, imposing Roman Christianity, and from Asia Minor into North Africa, imposing Islam and the destruction of "Kaffir" (pagan) monuments, temples and cultures which were seen as contradictory with the formation of a world dominated by Christianity, and later Islam.

Thus, even at the end of the 20th century the world is still contending with the agenda of some duplicitous or ignorant western scholars and writers of characterizing African culture as primitive and insignificant, and to elevate Western Culture and western scholarship without any footing in science. This is why the work of those who study Ancient Egyptian culture, religion and philosophy needs to confront the issue of history and the means to present evidences with rigorous standards that will lead to reasonable and useful conclusions, as opposed to disparaging remarks and insults calling the work of their opponents "wild", "flaky", "fantasies", opinion and innuendo.

Finally, this author (Ashby), knows of no African American Africentric scholar or African Africentric scholar who would say that Western civilization, as we know it today, is based on African civilization, it does however owe its existence to Ancient Africa since what the European countries built cannot be said to be in keeping with either the principles or philosophy of civilization enjoined by the Ancient Egyptian sages, nor the tenets that were learned by the Greek philosophers who were students of the Kamitan sages, who attempted to enlighten the early Greeks with the knowledge of the Land of the Pyramids. When asked by a western reporter what he thought about western civilization, the Indian leader Mahatma Ghandi is said to have replied: *"That is a good idea!"* He responded in this way because western civilization remains an idea yet to be realized. Technological advancement and material wealth or military power do not in themselves constitute "civilization." Western Culture cannot be considered to be a civilization since civilization means to be "civilized" in one's actions, constructions, and views towards the world. Being civilized means being civil (Civility = **1.** *Courteous behavior; politeness.* **2.** *A courteous act or utterance.* –American Heritage Dictionary) to other people. Civility is one of the most important concepts of Ancient Egyptian Maat philosophy. Being civilized does not mean just being courteous in social situations, but then taking advantage of the same people in another or promoting the welfare of one's own group, but promoting the welfare of all people in general, otherwise one's civilization is biased and therefore duplicitous and hypocritical, which disqualifies it from being regarded as a "civilization" in any stretch of the concept. Civilization benefits the world community as it sees all human beings as citizens of humanity. Being civilized cannot be equated with the denigration of women in the culture, the concept of a male god and the exclusion of women in religion, the global domination of people through economic manipulation and hoarding of resources, the enslavement of entire populations, the murder of entire populations and stealing their land, etc. These are not values of the ancient African culture, which was based on the principle of Humanism (Ubuntu/Maat) and required the provision of resources to meet the needs of all members of the population as well as the balance between male and female, etc. So Africa cannot be claimed to be the source of such acts of inhumanity, selfishness and greed. So wherever these were learned, they developed independently, perhaps due to the inability of people in Europe to heed the teachings of the Ancient Egyptian sages and their early Greek students. Thus, even though the early Greek philosophers created a spark in their home country that provided an impetus for the later development of European culture, that culture cannot yet be considered to be a civilization in the contexts of what was accomplished in Ancient Egypt (Africa).

References to the Nubian Genealogy of Kamitans in Kamitan Texts and Monuments

In the didactic treatise known as *The Prophesies of Neferti,* it is stated that Amunmhat I was the "son of a woman of Ta-Seti, a child of Upper Egypt. The term "Ta-Seti" means "Land of the Bow." This is one of the names used by the Ancient Egyptians to describe Nubia. Thus we are to understand that contrary to the assertions of orthodox Egyptologists, there are several Ancient Egyptian kings that can be recognized as "Nubian" besides those of the 25th dynasty. The late period Greeks and Romans referred to Pharaoh Amunhotep III {father of Amunhotep III – more commonly known as Akhenaton} (18th Dyn.) as Memnon, a Nubian, due to his appearance. They also accepted him as Pharaoh of Egypt. Yet there is a consistent effort to deny the obvious. When their histories and genealogies are examined, along with their statuary, it becomes clear that the Ancient Egyptians and their rulers were not just Africans but "black" skinned and also possessed the same physical features as other Africans. The two images below, of the same person [Above: Amenhotep III], demonstrate the difference between the naturalistic and the conventional {idealized-ritual} forms of depiction. These two forms should not be confused when determining the ethnic origins of the Ancient Egyptian images.

As Rome emerged as a powerful military force in the period just prior to the birth of Christ (200 B.C.E.-30 B.C.E.), they adopted Greek customs, religion and art, seeing these as their legacy. Just as the Greeks adopted *The Illiad* and *The Odyssey*, the Romans enthusiastically embraced *The Aeneid* as their national epic. Vergil or Virgil (70-19 B.C.E.) was a Roman poet who wrote *The Aeneid* in the Latin language.[14] *The Aeneid* is actually a story that was written in the same form as *The Odyssey* and *The Illiad* of the Greek writer Homer. It was widely distributed and read throughout the Roman Empire. Thus, *The Aeneid* is considered to be a classical Latin masterpiece of ancient world literature, which had enormous influence on later European writers.[15] Some portions of these texts have important implications to understand the relationship between the Egyptians, the Ethiopians and the Indians in ancient times. *(italicized portions are by Ashby)*

> Mixed in the bloody battle on the plain;
> ***And swarthy Memnon in his arms he knew,***
> ***His pompous ensigns, and his Indian crew.***
> - *The Aeneid*, Book I, Vergil or Virgil (70-19 BC)[16]

In Greek myth, Memnon was a king from Ethiopia, and was openly referred to as being "burnt of skin", i.e. "black."[i] He was the son of Tithonus, a Troyan (Trojan) prince, and Eos, a Greek goddess of the dawn. Tithonus and Eos represent the sky and romantic love, respectively. During the Troyan war, Memnon assisted Troy[17] with his army. Even though he fought valiantly, he was killed by Achilles. In order to comfort Memnon's mother, Zeus, the king of the Greek gods and goddesses, made Memnon immortal.[18] The Greeks revered a colossal statue of the Ancient Egyptian king Amenhotep III as an image of Memnon. During the times of Greek (332 B.C.E.-30 B.C.E.) and Roman (30 B.C.E.-450 A.C.E.) conquest of Egypt, it became fashionable for Greek and Roman royalty, nobles and those of means from all over the ancient world, especially Greece, to take sightseeing trips to Egypt. The "Colossi of Memnon" were big attractions. The Colossi of Memnon are two massive statues that were built under Amenhotep III, 1,417-1,379 B.C.E.[19] The statues fronted a large temple[20] which is now in ruin, mostly depleted of its stonework by nearby Arab inhabitants who used them to build houses.

---
[i] Recall that the term Ethiopians means "land of the burnt (black) faces."

This passage is very important because it establishes a connection between Ethiopia, Egypt and India. Further, it establishes that the Indians made up the army of Memnon, that is to say, Ethiopia. Thus, in the time of Virgil, the cultural relationship between north-east Africa and India was so well known that it was mythically carried back in time to the reign of Pharaoh Amenhotep III, the father of the famous king Akhnaton. Pharaoh Amenhotep III was one of the most successful kings of Ancient Egypt. He ruled the area from northern Sudan (Nubia) to the Euphrates river. The Euphrates river is formed by the confluence of the Murat Nehri and the Kara Su Rivers. It flows from East Turkey across Syria into central modern day Iraq where it joins the Tigris River. The land referred to as Mesopotamia, along the lower Euphrates, was the birthplace of the ancient civilizations of Babylonia and Assyria, and the site of the ancient cities of Sippar, Babylon, Erech, Larsa, and Ur. The length of the river is 2,235mi (3.598km).[21] So again we have support for the writings of Herodotus and Diodorus who related the makeup of the ethnic groups in Mesopotamia as belonging to the Ancient Egyptian-Nubian culture.

One issue that western and Arab scholars who want to characterize the appearance of "Nubian features" in Ancient Egyptian art is that these are either rare or that they appear almost exclusively in the period of the 25th Dynasty when it is universally accepted that the Nubians from the south took over the all of Egypt. However, a cursory study of the Ancient Egyptian statues and relief provides insights into the insufficiency of any arguments pretending to suggest that there are no records besides the Greek classical writers which show that the Ancient Egyptians saw and depicted themselves as "black Africans," not just during the 25th Dynasty, but throughout the history of Ancient Egypt to the Greek and Roman periods.

Below: Left- Peraah (Pharaoh) Muntuhotep II (Muntuhotep)[22] – 11th Dynasty

Below: Center- Peraah Senusert I statue – 12th Dynasty

Below: Right- Peraah Senusert I relief – 12th Dynasty

(A)   (B)   (C)

The images above are representative of the reliefs and statuaries that the Greek classical writers and the seventeenth- and eighteenth-century European travelers in Egypt saw in full color. Notice the features of the first two (A-B) faces. They clearly exhibit the characteristic traits that have been described as "Black African", including the "puffed up face." Plate (C) is actually a relief representing the same personality as plate (B). Notice that the features in the statues are more pronounced than in the reliefs. This same pattern of iconography can be observed in the statuary and reliefs of King Akhnaton. What we are witnessing is an Ancient Egyptian artistic standard practice of representing the personality in a more naturalistic form in the statuary, and a more standardized manner in the reliefs.[i] In all cases however, the features denote the "bloated face, puffed up eyes, flat nose, and thick lips, and woolly hair as well as the brown-red or black skin tone painting.

Pharaoh Muntuhotep II was a very important personality in the history of Ancient Egypt. His efforts completed the reunion of Egypt during the 11th Dynasty. The culture was revived, and the Pharaoh built a great temple consisting of two colonnaded terraces in a place in Egypt now called Deir el-Bahri, opposite Waset (Luxor) . Pharaoh Hatshepsut had a copy of this temple made alongside it several hundred years later, at an even greater scale.

The Middle Kingdom saw a return to peace and order. Egypt's borders were again expanded to include Asia Minor, central and eastern Asia and northern Nubia. Under Senusert I (Sesostris), Ancient Egyptian culture extended over a vast region. There was trade and expedition to other countries in the Mediterranean, as well as along the East Coast of Africa. Security measures including fortresses were constructed to repel future attacks.

The literature of the period consists of instructions (Wisdom Texts), prophecies and tales, such as the advice of the aged Amenemhat I to his son, as well as wisdom texts. The tales of the Shipwrecked Sailor, Sinuhe, and the Eloquent Peasant all derive from this time.[23]

There are definitely different facial features displayed in Ancient Egyptian iconographies. There are also different facial features in different parts of Africa. Yet the Greek descriptions most often mention features such as flat noses and thick lips when describing Ethiopians and Egyptians. The depiction of the physiognomy, in particular the nose, the lips and eye region of the face of most Ancient Egyptian sculptures prior to the Asiatic invasions depict clear "African features". In the ancient period the hair style also serves to depict typically African hair. There are statues from varied periods that can be examined, that demonstrate the African ethnicity of the Ancient Egyptians. The curly hair or hair in locks or braids was used in ancient Kamit and similar forms were used by the Buddhists.

Above left: Sculpture of an Ancient Egyptian Official from Sakkara (Old Kingdom) Brooklyn Museum
Above right: Kamitan-Kushitic sculpture, described by the Brooklyn Museum as "Black man."
(Hellenistic period)

---

[i] *The projection of figures or forms from a flat background, as in sculpture, or such a projection that is apparent only, as in painting.* – American Heritage Dictionary

The following images of the Ancient Egyptian King Akhenaton depict him in varied ways, A and C and D-as having distinctly African facial features; B- as the idealized Pharaoh, with Nubian features.

A-Below left, Per-aah Akhnaton Statue (18 Dynasty) – Cairo Museum

B-Below right, Per-aah Akhnaton Relief (18 Dynasty)

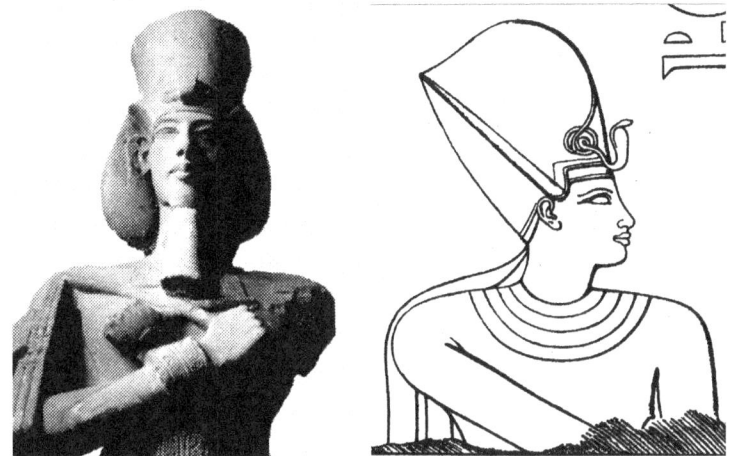

B- Akhnaton as Amunhotep 4th depicted conventionally

A & C- Akhnaton as Amunhotep 4th depicted naturalistically

C-Above: Akhenaton amidst the rays of Aton which are bringing life. ☥

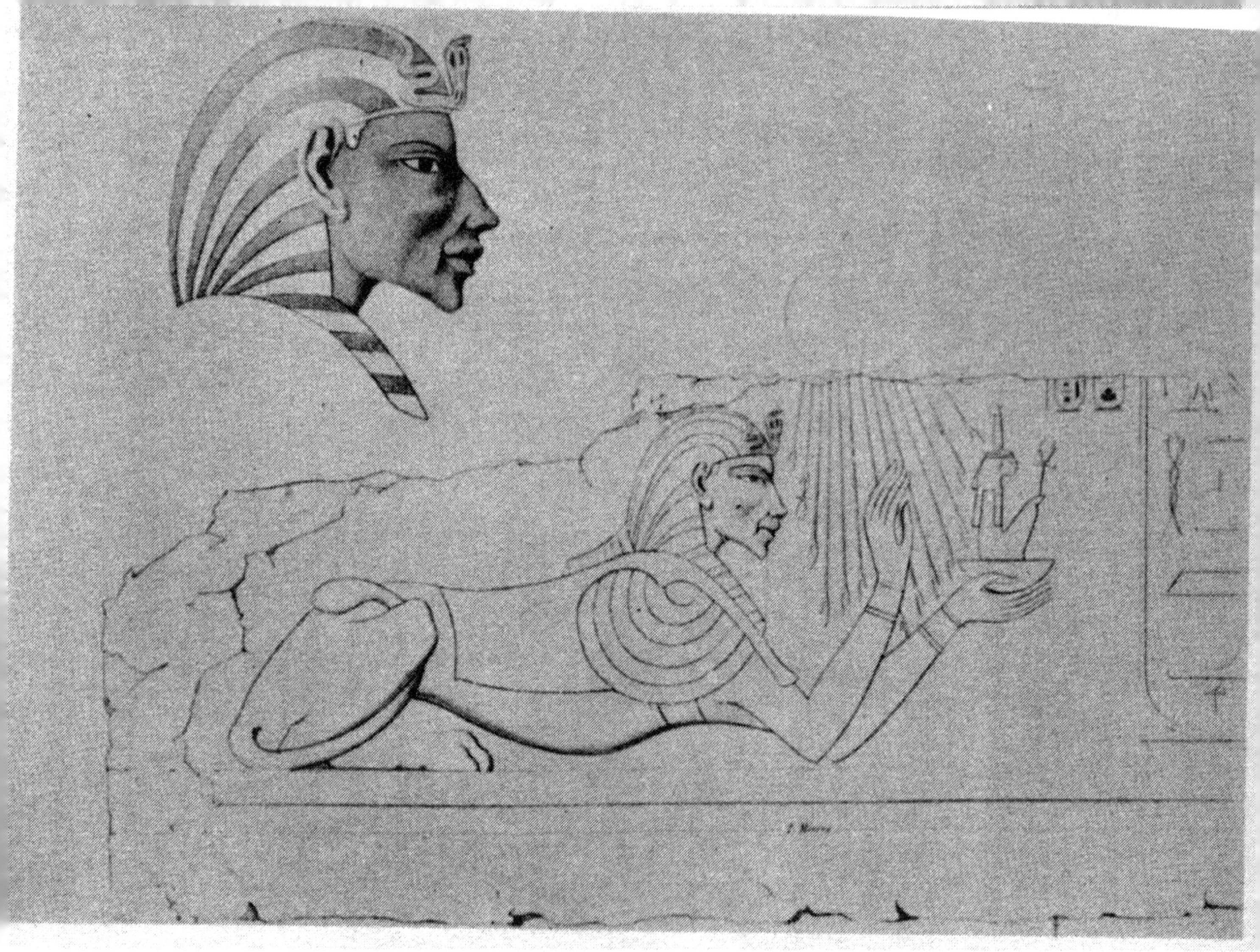

D-Above: Akhenaton as sphinx offering maat with rays

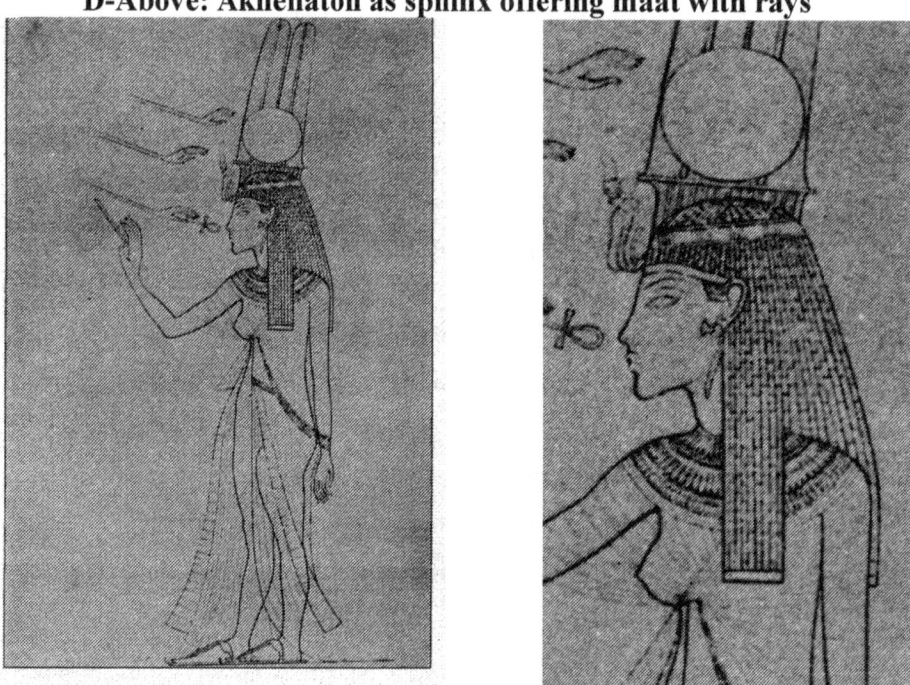

Above- Queen Ty, mother of Akhenaton receiving life from Aton rays.

Color Plates

Color Plate 1: Nubians (three figures prostrating) and Egyptians (standing figures) are depicted with the

Below: Complete scene

NUBIANS   NUBIANS   NUBIANS   NUBIANS   EGYPTIANS
same colors of their skin of alternating black and brown -Tomb of Huy

EGYPTIAN   NUBIANS

Per-aah (Pharaoh) Muntuhotep II (Muntuhotep)[i] – 11th Dynasty

Below: Nubians and Egyptians are depicted with the same colors of alternating black and brown -Tomb of Huy (image from drawing of 19th century explorers)

Color Plate 2: Ancient Egyptians and Nubians depicted in the Tomb of Rameses III

The Tomb of Seti I (1306-1290 B.C.E.-below) which comes earlier than that of Rameses III (above) shows a different depiction. Note that the same labels are used to describe the Egyptians and Nubians in the pictures of both tombs.

Color Plate 3: Ancient Egyptians and Nubians depicted in the Tomb of Seti I. Notice the similarity between the Nubian depiction below and the depictions from the Tomb of Huy (above).

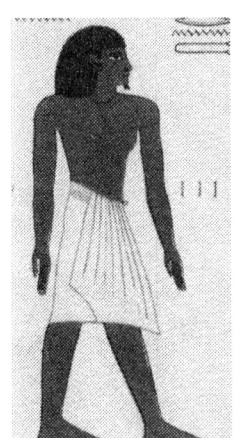 

Rtji **Ancient Egyptian**   *Ahsu* **Ancient Nubian**

The Black African Ancient Egyptians

Color Plate 4: Black and Red Pottery, Below left (A)- Painted Pottery from Mohenjodaro –Indus Valley, India[24]: Below right (B & C)- Painted Pottery from the Pre-Dynastic Period – Egypt Africa.[25]

(A) (B) (C)

Color Plate 5: Below left- Pottery Black and Red - from north and south India- c. 500 B.C.E. tomb at Manla Ali, Hyderabad (British Museum) – Below right- Black and Red pottery from Pre-Dynastic Egyptian burial now at Metropolitan Museum New York. Photos by M. Ashby.

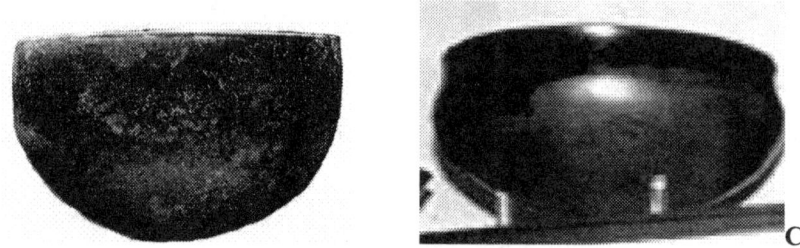

Color Plate 6 above right - Nubian depictions from Akhnaton period (1352 B.C.E-1347 B.C.E)

Above: Nubian from the Tomb of Rameses III

Philip Arrhidaeus, (top center) successor of Alexander, a Greek, in depicted in Red (From the Napoleonic Expedition)

Picture of a display at the Brooklyn Museum (1998-2000) showing the similarity between the headrest of Ancient Egypt (foreground) and those used in other parts of Africa (background). (Photo by M. Ashby)

On the following page: Ancient Egyptian Depiction of Ethnic Groups (New Kingdom Dynastic Period)[i] (Originally in the tomb of *Ramose* – drawn by Prisse d' Avennes) {-colorized version by Muata Ashby}

The Black African Ancient Egyptian

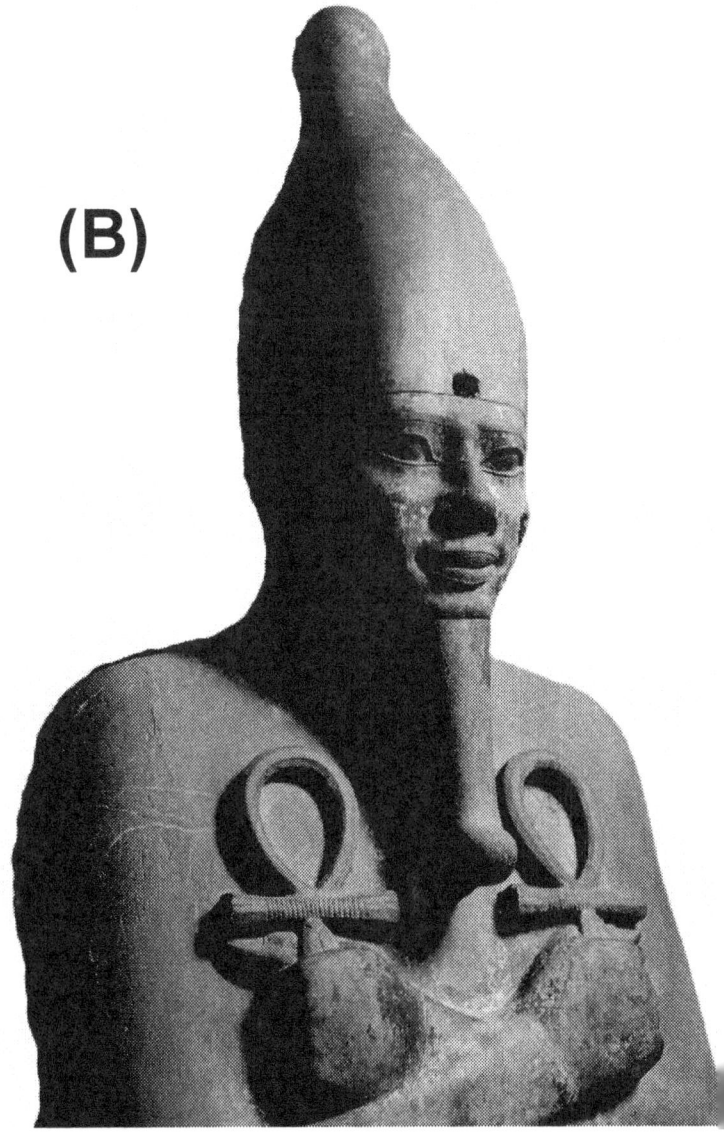

Plate 1: Left- <u>Peraah</u> (Pharaoh) Muntuhotep II (Muntuhotep) – 11th Dynasty
Plate 2: Center- Peraah Senusert I statue – 12th Dynasty
Plate 3: Right- Peraah Senusert I relief – 12th Dynasty

The Black African Ancient Egyptians

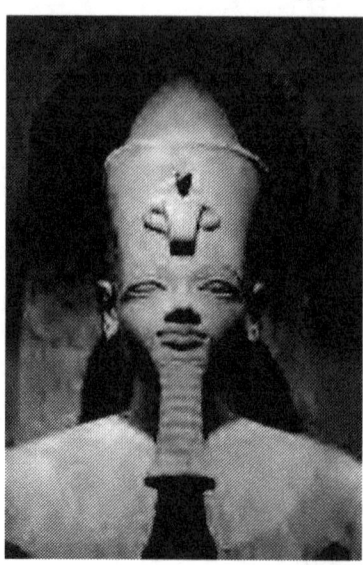

Above: Amenhotep III {sculpted in a naturalistic form-as he appeared in real life}

Below: Amenhotep III {sculpted in a conventional (idealized) form-as he is meant to appeared as Pharaoh}

On next two pages: another image of Amenhotep III {sculpted in a naturalistic form-as he appeared in real life} Next: image of Amunhotep IV (Akhenaton), the son of Amunhotep III

40

Senusert Statue from Cairo Museum

Senusert Statue from Cairo Museum

The picture above is a painted Limestone stela of chamberlain Amunemhat [12 Dynasty] which displays African features and skin color. [British Museum]

On next page: Statue of a Nubian king in Sudan, maybe it is king Natakamani. The statue was found in Tabo on the isle of Argo

Below left – late 20th century Nubian man. Below right-Nubian Prisoners of Rameses II -Image at the Abu Simbel Temple

Below: Bottom left-Ancient Egyptians (musicians) and Nubians (dancers) depicted in the Tombs of the Nobles with the same hue and features. Bottom right- Nubian King Taharka and the Queen offering to Amun (blue) and Mut (yellow) depicted as a red Egyptians. 7th cent BCE

Below-left, Egyptian man and woman-(tomb of Payry) 18th Dynasty displaying the naturalistic style (as people really appeared in ancient times). Below right- Egyptian man and woman-Theban tomb – displaying the colors red and yellow.

Below-left, Stele of Niptah - end of Middle Kingdom (man in red, woman in white with breasts exposed). Below right- Minoan man in red and Minoan woman in white with breasts exposed. (1400 B.C.E.).

The Black African Ancient Egyptians

Below: Images of Black (pictured in dark red in traditional Egyptian style) Skinned Ancient Egyptian being served by others. Sarcofagus of Ashayt, 2060-2010 B.C.E.

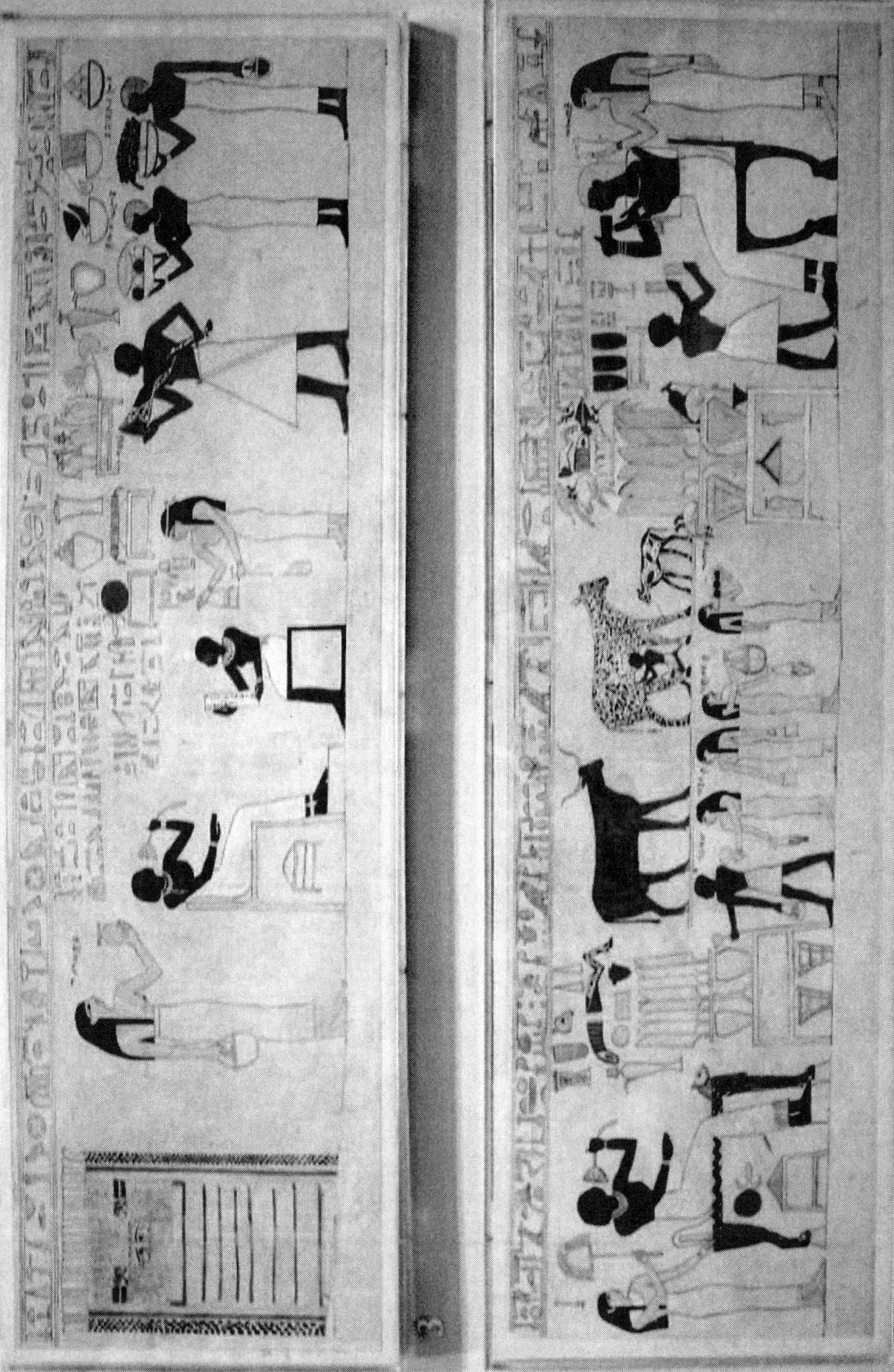

The Black African Ancient Egyptians

Below: Three Images of Greco-Roman Egyptians as they had themselves pictured on their coffins.

The Black African Ancient Egyptians

The Black African Ancient Egyptians
Two Images of Queen Hatshepsut displayed in a naturalistic form (As she looked in real life)

Images on this page: Images of Queen Hatshepsut as Pharaoh depicted in conventional-idealistic form exemplifying the epitome of perfection.

Painting of the Great Sphinx while buried up to its neck, by Denon 19 century

Photograph of the Sphinx while buried up to its neck – 19th Century.

On the following page- the Great Phinx – late 20th century. – after modern restorations

How Some Western and Arab Scholars Distort Evidence Pointing to the Older Age of Ancient Egyptian Culture

After examining the writings of many Western scholars, the feeling of many Africentrists and Africologists (researchers into African culture) of African descent and some non-African Western scholars is that traditional Egyptologists, a group comprised almost entirely of people of European descent or who have been trained by Western scholars, have over the years sought to bring down the estimated date for the commencement of the Dynastic Period in Egypt in order to show that Ancient Egyptian culture emerged after Mesopotamian culture. Presumably, this was done because Mesopotamia is held by many Western scholars to be their (Western Culture's) own, if not genetic, cultural ancestral homeland. The reader should understand the context of this issue that goes to the heart of cultural relations between Western Culture and Eastern and African cultures. From the perspective of many people of non-European descent, Western Culture has sought to establish its socio-economic supremacy by suppressing and undermining the capacity of indigenous peoples worldwide, to govern themselves and control their own resources. This is verified by the documented evidence of the African slave trade,[26] military and covert intervention to destabilize governments, distortion of history,[27\28] colonial and neocolonial systems,[29] etc., either set up or supported by Western countries in the past 500 years. In order to perpetuate this control, the image of superiority demands that Western Culture should be able to project an ancestral right, as it were, to control other countries. Therefore, twisting evidence in order to make Western Culture appear ancient, wise, beneficial, etc., necessitates a denial that there is any civilization that is older or possibly better than Western civilization, or that there could be any genetic or cultural relation with the non-Western Cultures which are being subjugated, or a common ancestry with the rest of humanity. An example of this twisting of history by Western scholars is the well known and documented deliberate misinterpretation of the Biblical story of Noah, so as to make it appear that the Bible advocated and condones the enslavement of the children (descendants) of Ham (all Hamitic peoples- people of African descent) by the children (descendants) of Japheth (all peoples of Germanic {European} descent).

Along with the natural stubbornness of ordinary human beings to accept change due to the their identification with prestige of their culture and heritage as a source of self-worth instead of truth and virtue, two methods of discrediting the early achievements of Ancient Egypt have been used.

The desire of Western Culture to envision their own history as a civilized culture stretching back into antiquity, having realized that Greek culture is too late in history to establish this claim, and not wanting to acknowledge that Ancient Greece essentially owes[30] its civilization to Ancient Egypt,[31] have promoted a process of downplaying the importance of Ancient Egypt in history, by means of reducing the chronology in which history took place. How could this obfuscation of the record occur?

In addition to the resistance by some in Western scholars to accept information, which they fear, will change the prestige of their culture and heritage with which they identify as a source of their self-worth, instead of defining themselves by the standards of truth and virtue, other methods of discrediting the early achievements of Ancient Egypt have been used. Two ways of invalidating Ancient Egyptian history are prominent: 1- misunderstanding or 2- supporting erroneous theories.

One method used by Western Egyptologists to contradict Kamitan history was to examine surviving[i] Ancient Egyptian mummies and apply undetermined forensic techniques in order to assign "causes of death" to the entire Ancient Egyptian culture. From this they concluded that the Ancient Egyptians had a short life span due to "primitive living conditions," and that the average life expectancy of a Pharaoh being no more than 20 years or so. However, since the cause of death can often not be determined even in modern times, how can the results derived from any technique(s) being applied to a 3,000 + years old mummified body be conclusive? When such rationales are not considered, and the erroneous pronouncements repeated over and over again, they become "accepted" as truth by scholars and lay persons for a variety of reasons, some of which we have already touched on above. The problem becomes compounded because many scholars and lay people alike do not do their own research or look at the evidence themselves and draw their own conclusions. Rather, they are comfortable accepting the information being provided, without questioning its validity. Some don't want to know, because they do not want to risk their positions by disrupting the status quo. Others may be unwilling, or unable due to blind faith and mental weakness, to examine the evidences. In addition, there are other factors to be considered such as socio-economic obstacles, physical barriers preventing access to information, training, etc.

Another method used to revise the history of the Dynastic Period in Kamit is to say that the kings or queens were ruling concurrently in certain periods as opposed to subsequently. In certain periods such as the invasion of the Hyksos and the Assyrians, Persians, etc. who conquered part of the country, Egyptian leaders ruled in their part of the country while the conquerors temporarily ruled the conquered territory that they captured. Also, this is possible in the Intermediate period when there was a partial breakdown of social order. Further, due to the destruction of records, there are many Ancient Egyptian rulers (kings and queens) mentioned whose names are no longer recorded. (See the Ancient Egyptian King and Queen List in Appendix A)

Since we have lists of the Pharaohs of the Dynastic Period, we can easily count the number of Pharaohs and use this figure to estimate what the average life span of each Pharaoh would have to be to cover the time span of the Dynastic Period, which lasted approximately 3,000 + years. Doing the math by multiplying this number by the life expectancy proposed by scholars (20 years), one arrives at a figure that is less than 3,000 years, the duration of the Dynastic period. Also, the conclusion drawn from the above methodology used to estimate the life span of the Kamitan peoples from mummified bodies (of the average life span of 20 years), even if it were accurate, does not make sense if we consider the ample documentation showing that Ancient Egypt was reputed to have the "best doctors" in the ancient world. Further, even if it were true that ordinary people existed in "primitive living conditions," does it make sense that the kings and queens would get the worst health care out of the entire population? Thus, as a scholar, is it prudent to apply this number to the royalty? Also, there is documented evidence to show that kings and queens, as well as other members of the society, lived normal healthy lives by modern

---
[i] Many mummies have been destroyed throughout history by the early Christians and Muslims who wanted to eradicate all records of religions existing prior to their own, and also early European explorers who sold the mummies for experimentation as well as other Europeans who created a fad of pulverizing the mummies and using them in potions as medicinal supplements.

standards. There are surviving records and statues, as well as illustrations, of kings, mummies and other royalty who lived well into their 80's and 90's such as Amunhotep Son of Hapu and Rameses II and others. One might also envision the wretchedness of such a life where members of a society die at such an early age. No sooner does one realize the potential of life, than one dies, as a mere child. Life would hardly be worth living. Also, since spiritual evolution requires maturity in ordinary human terms, that is, sufficient time to grow up and discover the meaning of life, a short life-span would make the vast number of extant Kamitan texts treating the subject of spiritual enlightenment impossible to create, and useless because there would not be sufficient time to take advantage of them.

Another method used to discredit the Kamitan history is to arbitrarily claim that when the Ancient Egyptians spoke of "years," they were actually referring to "months".[32] This practice is predicated on baseless supposition, and is therefore, patently false and demeaning since there is no precedent for this practice in Ancient Egyptian culture. It is an imaginary notion introduced by some Egyptologists who prefer to fantasize rather than face the magnitude of their discoveries. Thus, the corrupt nature of the historians, scholars and those who perpetuate such iniquitous misrepresentations is evident.

Still another motivation has been to try to synchronize the events such as those described in Ancient Egyptian texts or the Greek histories with those of the Bible. An example of this kind of writing can be found in a book by W. G. Waddell, called *Manetho*. Some historians feel this kind of distortion was done to establish the prestige of the Judeo-Christian tradition, the reasoning being similar to that discussed above. They believe that Judeo-Christian view was that having other traditions that are recognized as older and having more honor, heritage and prominence would undermine the perception that the Bible is ancient and infallible.

Others feel the reason was out of an effort to prove that Ancient Egyptian culture existed within the timeframe that the Bible has posed for the Creation of the world. The Creation was dated by the 17th-century[i] Irish archbishop James Ussher to have occurred in the year 4004 B.C.E.[33] If the world is approximately 6,005[ii] years old, as postulated by the archbishop, this would support the teaching presented in the church and invalidate the existence of culture, philosophy, and most of all, religion, prior to the emergence of Christianity.

The work of Darwin (theory of evolution) and other scientists caused major controversies in western society. A case in point is the attempt to correlate the events of the Biblical story of Exodus with those of Ancient Egyptian Pharaoh, Rameses II. First, there are no accounts of any conflict between the Jews and the Egyptians in any Ancient Egyptian records yet discovered, beyond an inscription at the Karnak temple in Egypt stating that the Jews were one of the tribes under Egyptian rule in Palestine. Secondly, there are no corroborating records of the events chronicled in the Bible in any of the contemporary writings from countries that had contact with the Jews and the Ancient Egyptians. Thirdly, there were at least eleven kings who went by the title Rameses (Rameses I, II, III, III, etc.), spanning a period dated by traditional Egyptologists from 1,307 B.C.E. to 1,070 B.C.E. Further, some localities were also referred to as Rameses.

The oldest scholarly dating for the existence of Moses, if he did exist, is c. 1,200 B.C.E. However, most Bible scholars agree that the earliest texts of the Bible were composed around 1,000 B.C.E or later, and were developed over the next millennia. Also, most scholars are now

---

[i] 17th century refers to the time period from 1,600-1,699 A.C.E.
[ii] 4,004 + 1,600 to1,699 gives a range of time span from 4,604-5,703; this has been conservatively rounded to 6,000.

beginning to accept the Ancient Egyptian and therefore, African ethnicity of the original Jewish peoples. An example of modern scholarship on the question of the origins of the Jews occurs in the book *Bible Myth: The African Origins of the Jewish People*. In a section entitled "Contradictory Biblical Evidence," the author, Gary Greenberg states:

> Dating the Exodus is problematic because evidence of its occurrence appears exclusively in the Bible, and what little it tells is contradictory. Exodus 12:40-41, for example, places the Exodus 430 years after the start of Israel's sojourn in Egypt (i.e., beginning with Jacob's arrival), whereas Genesis 15:13-14 indicates that four hundred years transpired from the birth of Isaac to the end of the bondage. Both claims cannot be true. Jacob was born in Isaac's 60th year,[34] and he didn't arrive in Egypt until his 130th year.[35] If the sojourn lasted 430 years, then the Exodus would have to have occurred 620 years after Isaac's birth.[36] On the other hand, if the Exodus occurred 400 years after Isaac was born, then the sojourn could only have been 210 years long.[37] Other biblical passages raise additional problems.[38]

The story of Sargon I points to another source and purpose for the Moses story, in our present context. According to the Biblical tradition, at about 1200? B.C.E., the Hebrews were in Egypt, serving as slaves. A Jewish woman placed her son in a basket and allowed it to float downstream where the Egyptian queen found it, and then adopted the child. The child was Moses, the chosen one of God, who would lead the Jews out of bondage in Egypt. Moses was taken in by the royal family and taught the wisdom related to rulership of the nation as well as to the Egyptian religion and the Egyptian Temples (Bible: Acts 7:22). He was being groomed to be king and high priest of Egypt. This is why the Bible says he was knowledgeable in the wisdom of the Egyptians (Bible: Acts 7:22 and Koran C.144: Verses 37 to 76).

A story similar to the birth of Moses, about a child being placed in a basket and put in a stream which was later found by a queen, can be found in Zoroastrian mythology as well.[58] Also, recall the Semitic ruler, Sargon I, was rescued in the same manner after he was placed in a basket and sent floating down a river. Sargon I reined about 2,335-2,279 B.C.E. He was called "Sargon, The Great." He was one of the first known major Semitic conquerors in history. He was successful in conquering the entire country of Sumer, an ancient country of southwestern Asia, which corresponds approximately to the biblical land known as Babylonia (Babylon). Babylon was an ancient city of Mesopotamia, which was located on the Euphrates River about 55mi (89km) South of present-day Baghdad. Sargon I created an empire stretching from the Mediterranean to the Persian Gulf in c. 2,350 B.C.E. The adoption of the child into royalty and rulership motif was apparently a popular theme in ancient times for those who wanted to legitimize their ascendancy to power by creating the perception that it was divinely ordained.[39]

Despite the myriad of ongoing excavations that have been conducted, many sponsored by Christian or Jewish groups, no substantial evidence has been unearthed that supports the historicity of the Bible. However, new discoveries have been brought forth that corroborate Herodotus' statements and the histories relating to the fact that the land that is now called Palestine, was once part of Ancient Egypt.

> An approximately 5,000-year-old settlement discovered in southern Israel was built and ruled by Egyptians during the formative period of Egyptian civilization, a team of archaeologists announced last week.

The new find, which includes the first Egyptian-style tomb known to have existed in Israel at that time, suggests that ancient Egypt exerted more control over neighboring regions than investigators have often assumed, contends project director Thomas E. Levy of the University of California, San Diego.

> Source: Science News, Oct 5, 1996 v150 n14 p215(1).
> Title: Ancient Egyptian outpost found in Israel.
> (Halif Terrace site in southern Israel upsets
> previous estimates of Egyptian imperialism) Author: Bruce Bower

Speaking out against the stronghold, which modern European and American Egyptologists have created, the Egyptologist, scholar and author, John Anthony West, detailed his experiences and those of others attempting to study the Ancient Egyptian monuments and artifacts who are not part of the "accepted" Egyptological clique. He describes the situation as a kind of "Fortress Egypt." He describes the manner in which, not only are the Ancient Egyptian artifacts closely protected from the examination of anyone outside this group, but also the interpretation of them as well. It is as if there is a propaganda machine, which, like the orthodox medical establishment, has set itself up as sole purveyors of the "correct" knowledge in the field, and thereby invalidates the findings of other scholars or scientists. In discussing the way in which mistakes made by scholars are treated, Mister West says the following:

> In academia, the rules vis-à-vis mistakes change according to location. Only those within the establishment are allowed to 'make mistakes.' Everyone else is a 'crank' 'crackpot' or 'charlatan,' and entire lifetimes of work are discredited or dismissed on the basis of minor errors.

Also, the treatment of any scholar who reads metaphysical import in the teachings, literature or iconography of Ancient Egypt is generally ridiculed by orthodox Egyptologists. For instance, anyone suggesting that the Great pyramids were not used as burial chambers (mummies or remnants of mummies have never been discovered in them), but rather as temples, is openly called a "Pyramidiot,"[40] West describes the ominous power that orthodox Egyptologists have taken to themselves and the danger this power poses to humanity:

> A tacit territorial agreement prevails throughout all Academia. Biochemists steer clear of sociology; Shakespearean scholars do not disparage radio astronomy. It's taken for granted that each discipline, scientific, scholarly or humanistic, has its own valid self-policing system, and that academic credentials ensure expertise in a given field.
> With its jealous monopoly on the impenetrable hieroglyphs,± its closed ranks, restricted membership, landlocked philosophical vistas, empty coffers, and its lack of impact upon virtually every other academic, scientific or humanistic field, Egyptology has prepared a near-impregnable strategic position for itself - an academic Switzerland but without chocolate, cuckoo clocks, scenery or ski slopes, and cannily concealing its banks. Not only is it indescribably boring and difficult to attack, who'd want to?
> But if Swiss financiers suddenly decided to jam the world's banking system, Swiss neutrality and impregnability might suddenly be at risk. That is partially analogous to the situation of Egyptology. The gold is there, but its existence is denied, and no one is allowed to inspect the vaults except those whose credentials

make them privy to the conspiracy and guarantee their silence. To date, only a handful of astute but powerless outsiders have recognized that the situation poses real danger. But it's not easy to generate a widespread awareness or appreciation of that danger.

If you think of Egyptologists at all, the chances are you conjure up a bunch of harmless pedants, supervising remote desert digs or sequestered away in libraries, up to their elbows in old papyrus. You don't think of them as sinister, or dangerous. The illuminati responsible for the hydrogen bomb, nerve gas and Agent Orange are dangerous; if you reflect upon it you see that the advanced beings who have given us striped toothpaste and disposable diapers are also dangerous ... but Egyptologists?

Possibly they are the most dangerous of all; dangerous because false ideas are dangerous. At any rate *some* false ideas are dangerous. Belief in the flat earth never hurt anyone though it made navigation problematic. Belief in a geocentric universe held back advances in astronomy but otherwise had certain metaphysical advantages. Academic Egyptology is dangerous because it maintains, in spite of Schwaller de Lubicz's documented scholarly evidence, and the obvious evidence of our own eyes and hearts when we go there, that the race responsible for the pyramids and the temples of Karnak and Luxor was less, 'advanced' than ourselves. As long as academic Egyptology prevails, children will be brought up with a totally distorted view of our human past, and by extension, of our human present. And millions of tourists will continue to visit Egypt every year, and have the experience of a lifetime vitiated and subverted by a banal explanation that the greatest art and architecture in the world to superstitious primitives.

So the fabulous metaphysical gold of Egypt remains hidden; it's existence stridently denied. For orthodox Egyptology is really little more than a covert operation within the Church of Progress. Its unspoken agenda is to maintain the faith; not to study or debate the truth about Egypt.[1]

±NOTE (by West): Who will claim authority to challenge the accepted translations of the texts, even when these read as nonsense? Actually, a number of independent scholars have learned the hieroglyphs for themselves and produced alternative less insulting translations of some of the texts. But since these are either ignored or dismissed out of hand by orthodox Egyptologists, there is no way to know if these translations come closer to the real thinking of the ancients or if they are themselves no more than figments of the translators' imaginations, and in consequence no more representative and satisfactory than the standard translations.

Noting further difficulties of sustaining independent or "alternative" Egyptology studies, West remains hopeful that the pressure to revise their unsupportable findings, not just from alternative Egyptologists, but also from geologists who bring to bear an irrefutable and exacting science to the dating of Ancient Egyptian monuments as opposed to the methods which other reputable sociologists and historians have found to be unreliable. Of the major methods accepted for establishing a chronology to understand the origins of civilization and the history of the world such as Astronomical Time, Geological Time, Archaeological Time and Political or Historical Time, the use of Scriptural chronology is recognized as being "extremely uncertain

---

[1] *Serpent in the Sky,* John Anthony West, p. 239

because various local chronologies were used at different times by scriptural writers, and different systems were used by contemporaneous writers."[i]

> An alternative Egyptology is less easily managed. Almost no one can earn a living from it. Serious research is difficult to accomplish on a spare-time basis, and research requires access to the few major Egyptological libraries scattered around the world. In Egypt itself, excavation and all work on or in the pyramids, temples and tombs are controlled by the Egyptian Antiquities Organizations. No one without academic credentials can expect to obtain permission to carry out original work[ii] Infiltration from within is also peculiarly difficult. At least a few people I know personally have set out to acquire degrees in Egyptology, hoping to devote themselves full time to Egypt and ultimately to legitimize the symbolist interpretation. So far, none have been able to stick out the boredom or dutifully parrot the party line for the years necessary to get the diploma, knowing better from the onset.
>
> It seems unlikely that symbolist Egypt will ever establish itself from within its own ranks. But pressure from outside Egyptology but within academia could force a change. Academics with an interest but no personal stake in the matter must sooner or later realize that the support of highly qualified geologists (of a fundamentally geological theory) must overrule either the clamor or the silence of the Egyptological/archeological establishment. At some point they must express those views.[iii]

Having read the preceding excerpts published in 1993 by West, one might think that orthodox Egyptology has never been successfully challenged. African, African American and other African Egyptologists in the Diaspora faced the same problem when they brought forth evidences, which proved that the Ancient Egyptian civilization was originally created by African people, and that people of African descent played a crucial role in the development of Ancient Egyptian culture and its interactions with other world cultures. This engendered a major storm of repudiation and ridicule beginning in the 1970's. African, African American and other African scholars and Egyptologists in the Diaspora such as Chancellor Williams, George G. M. James, John H. Clarke, Yosef A. A. Ben-jochannan[41] and Cheikh Anta Diop[42] were denigrated, and their struggle to be heard even in their own communities was hampered by the constant rhetoric and derision from orthodox Egyptologists. Catching orthodox Egyptology by surprise, however, Cheikh Anta Diop not only challenged their opinion about the African origins of Ancient Egyptian culture, religion and philosophy, but offered overwhelming proof to support his contentions at the 1974 Unesco conference in which he faced 18 of the (at that time) leaders of the orthodox Egyptological community. Describing the evidence presented at the Unesco

---

[i] "Chronology," Microsoft (R) Encarta Encyclopedia. Copyright (c) 1994
[ii] West adds the following footnote: Prior to the development of modern day Egyptology by the western nations, native Egyptians showed little regard or respect for their distant dynastic ancestors; the temples were quarried for stone, anything movable was cheerfully sold to antiquities dealers. Islam, along with Christianity and Judaism, tended to regard ancient Egypt as pagan and idolatrous. But today, at least in private, Egyptian Egyptologists often display a much higher degree of understanding and sensitivity toward the Pharaonic achievement than their European and American colleagues. It would not surprise me to find some closet symbolists among them. Egyptian licensed tour guides (a much coveted job) must have degrees in academic Egyptology and pass an exacting test to qualify. Over the course of years of research and leading tours myself, at least a few dozen have approached me, eager to learn more about symbolist Egypt. But within the closed ranks of practicing, professional Egyptology, academic prestige (such as it is) is still wielded by the major European and American Universities. So even though all ancient Egyptian sites are now entirely under Egyptian control, an Egyptian Egyptologist would be as unlikely to try to break the "common front of silence" as anyone else, whatever his or her private convictions."
[iii] *Serpent in the Sky,* John Anthony West, p. 241

conference, scholar Asa G. Hilliard, described the proceedings as recorded by a news media reporter.[i]

In a scientific forum such opinions are unlikely to be expressed, they will be unable to compete with data-based arguments for, example, Dr. Diop presented eleven categories of evidence to support his argument for a native black African KMT[ii], including eye witness testimony of classical writers, melanin levels in the skin of mummies, Bible history, linguistic and cultural comparisons with the rest of Africa, Kamitan self descriptions, Kamitan historical references, physical anthropology data, blood type studies, carvings and paintings, etc.[iii] That is why the reporter at the Cairo Symposium wrote the following in the minutes of the meeting:

> "Although the preparatory working paper ... sent out by UNESCO gave particulars of what was desired, not all participants had prepared communications comparable with the painstakingly researched contributions of Professors Cheikh Anta Diop and Obenga. There was consequently a real lack of balance in the discussions."[iv]

At this conference, there was either expressed or implied consensus on the following points. (No objections were raised to them.)

1. In ancient KMT the south and the north were always ethnically homogeneous.
2. Professor Vercoutter's suggestion that the population of KMT had been made up of "black skinned whites" was treated as trivia.
3. There were no data presented to show that Kamitan temperament and thought were related to Mesopotamia.
4. The old Kamitan tradition speaks of the Great Lakes region in inner equatorial Africa as being the home of the ancient Kamitans.
5. There was no evidence of large-scale migration between Kamit and Mesopotamia. There were no Mesopotamian loan words in Kamitan: (therefore the two cultures could have no genetic linguistic relationship or be populated by the same people.) For comparison purposes, mention was made of the fact that when documented contact with Kamit was made by Asian Hyksos around 1700 B.C.E., loan words were left in ancient Kamit.
6. No empirical data were presented at the conference to show that the ancient Kemites were white. (Generally, there is a tendency for

---

[i] *Egypt Child of Africa* Edited by Ivan Van Sertima, *Bringing Maat, Destroying Isfet: The African and African Diasporan Presence in the Study of Ancient KMT* by Asa G. Hilliard III
[ii] Kamit (Ancient Egypt)
[iii] Diop, Cheikh Anta (1981) "Origin of the ancient Egyptians" In Moktar, G. *(Ed.) General history of Africa: volume II, Ancient Civilizations of Africa.* Berkeley, California: University of California Press, pp. 27-57
[iv] UNESCO, (1978) *The peopling of ancient Egypt and the deciphering of Meroitic script: The general history of Africa, studies and documents I, Proceedings of the symposium held in Cairo from 28 January to 3 February, 1974.* Paris: United Nations Educational, Scientific and Cultural Organization, p. 102.

some historians to *assume* that developed populations are white, but to require proof of blackness.)
7. Muslim Arabs conquered Kamit during the 7th century of the Common Era. Therefore, Arabic culture is not a part of Kamit during any part of the 3,000 years of dynastic Kamit.
8. Genetic linguistic relationships exist between the African languages of Kamitan, Cushitic (Ethiopian), Puanite (Punt or Somaliland), Berber, Chadic and Arabic. Arabic only covered territory off the continent of Africa, mainly in adjacent Saudi Arabia, an area in ancient times that was as much African as Asian.
9. Dr. Diop invented a melanin dosage test and applied it to royal mummies in the Museum of Man in Paris, mummies from the Marietta Excavations. All had melanin levels consistent with a "black" population. The symposium participants made a strong recommendation that all royal mummies be tested. To date there is no word that this has been done. Dr. Diop struggled for the remaining years of his life to have access to the Cairo museum for that purpose, but to no avail.

Hilliard Concludes:

> Significantly, it was at the urging of African scholars, led by Dr. Cheikh Anta Diop, that this UNESCO sponsored scientific gathering was convened. Interestingly, the reporter's comments quoted above actually used one of the aspects of MAAT, "balance," to describe Diop and Obenga's work. Truly open dialogue brings MAAT and destroys ISFET[i]. We know this but have not required the open dialogue.

---

[i] unrighteousness

Mysticism of Color in Ancient Egyptian Art

Many Egyptologists and others have tried to put forth the idea that the reddish-brown (males) and yellow or white (for females) colors, which the Ancient Egyptians used in the artistic renditions of themselves, represented the hue of their skin. This argument is bogus since it is well known that if two people of different skin colors (pigmentation) mate, they will produce offspring displaying a mixture of the two hues, as well as a range of skin pigmentation hues which may extend even beyond the ranges represented by the parents, if the grandparents or those of even earlier generations were of different skin hues. So even if the Ancient Egyptians had consisted of a population of red men and yellow or white women, they would quickly transform themselves into pink and gold since red and yellow produces gold and red and white produces pink. Further, these mixtures would further combine until eventually only one hue would remain.

The color spectrum ranges, in order, from violet, through blue, green, yellow, and orange, to red.[43] The colors red and white hold special mystical significance, and this is why we see so many Ancient Egyptian couples represented by them, with the men painted reddish-brown and the women painted yellow or fully white. In color therapy, an art practiced in modern times as well as in Ancient Egypt,[44] the color red is understood as being an agitating or exciting (stimulating) color to the mind. White, on the other hand was considered in Ancient Egypt as soothing,[45] as the red male Hippo was considered violent, mischievous and destructive while the female was considered calm and helpful. Blue is considered as being soothing and relaxing to the mind. Mystically, red and white complement each other, as red symbolizes sexual potency or virility, and white, having the capacity to reflect all colors,[46] symbolizes pregnancy and potential. This is why the Kamitan Peraahs (Pharaohs)[i] wears the double crown, consisting of red and white elements. Note that when considering the colors from a scientific standpoint, and their effect on the human mind we obtain meanings that is not to be ascribed to the modern concept of race and racism. The colors do not refer to races but to energies and behavior patterns.

Mystically, the color gold symbolizes the sun and the spirit, as well as eternity and immortality. The color black symbolizes "the source" of all things, as it represents the capacity to absorb all colors."[47] Everything in Creation has color, in order to be seen. Black does not reflect any color due to its subtlety, thus it is "colorless," that is, uncolored by time and space, the realm (of Creation, duality and conditioning) where color exists. Another way to understand this is that black absorbs all colors, and does not let their light escape and white is opaque and thereby reflects all colors off itself, which is why movies use a white screen instead of black. This is why in mystical mythological philosophies of Kamit and India, the gods Asar and Amun in Ancient Egypt and the gods Vishnu and Krishna in India are referred to as the "black" ones. Amun and Krishna are also represented as dark blue. They represent the transcendent, beyond ordinary consciousness. Asar also symbolizes "nothingness." This is an allusion to the mind when it is void of concepts or thoughts. This spiritual idea is akin to the term "Shunya" used to describe the void that an aspirant strives to achieve in Buddhism.

---

[i] The term "Pharaoh" is a biblical (Hebrew-Jewish) translation oh the original Ancient Egyptian word "Per-aah".

Red + White thus means: Spirit + Matter = Creation. Thus these colors lead to productions (creations) in time and space as well as perfection in the physical plane.

Red + Yellow = Orange-Gold thus means: Spirit + Sublimated Matter = Eternity. Therefore these colors make each other whole and transcendental, i.e. symbolizing the movement from duality to non-duality.

Gold = Spirit and Eternity

Blue → moving towards Violet → leads to Black

Black = Transcendent

The Terms Kamit, "Ethiopia," "Nubia," "Kush" and "Sudan"

The term "Ethiopian," "Nubian," and "Kushite" all relate to the same peoples who lived south of Egypt. In modern times, the land which was once known as Nubia ("Land of Gold"), is currently known as the Sudan, and the land even further south and east towards the coast of east Africa is referred to as Ethiopia (see map above).

Recent research has shown that the modern Nubian word kiji means "fertile land, dark gray mud, silt, or black land." Since the sound of this word is close to the Ancient Egyptian name Kish or Kush, referring to the land south of Egypt, it is believed that the name Kush also meant "the land of dark silt" or "the black land." Kush was the Ancient Egyptian name for Nubia. Nubia, the black land, is the Sudan of today. Sudan is an Arabic translation of sûd which is the plural form of aswad, which means "black," and ân which means "of the." So, Sudan means "of the blacks." In the modern Nubian language, nugud means "black." Also, nuger, nugur, and nubi mean "black" as well. All of this indicates that the words Kush, Nubia, and Sudan all mean the same thing — the "black land" and/or the "land of the blacks."i As we will see, the differences between the term Kush and the term Kam (Qamit, Kamit, Kemit - name for Ancient Egypt in the Ancient Egyptian language) relate more to the same meaning but different geographical locations.

The Term Kamit (Qamit, Kamit, Kamit) and Its Relation to Nubia and the term "Black"

As we have seen, the terms "Ethiopia," "Nubia," "Kush" and "Sudan" all refer to "black land" and/or the "land of the blacks." In the same manner we find that the name of Egypt which was used by the Ancient Egyptians also means "black land" and/or the "land of the blacks." The hieroglyphs below reveal the Ancient Egyptian meaning of the words related to the name of their land. It is clear that the meaning of the word Qamit is equivalent to the word Kush as far as they relate to "black land" and that they also refer to a differentiation in geographical location, i.e. Kush is the "black land of the south" and Qamit is the "black land of the north." Both terms denote the primary quality that defines Africa, "black" or "Blackness" (referring to the land and its people). The quality of blackness and the consonantal sound of K or Q as well as the reference to the land are all aspects of commonality between the Ancient Kushitic and Kamitan terms.

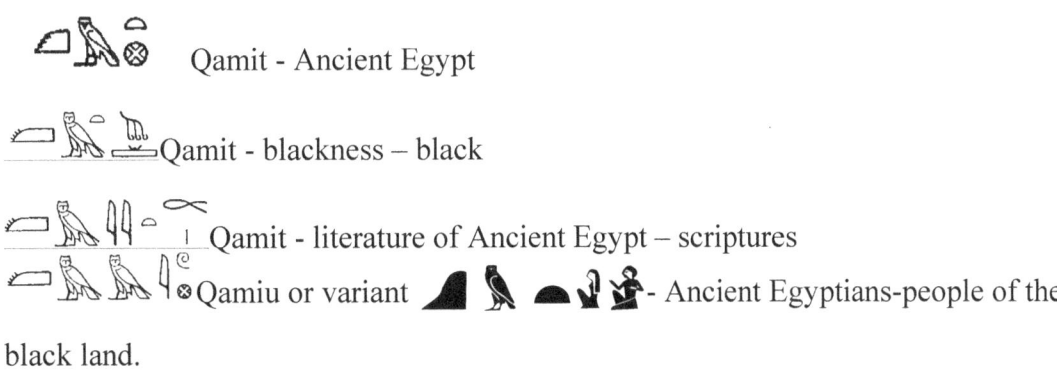

Qamit - Ancient Egypt

Qamit - blackness – black

Qamit - literature of Ancient Egypt – scriptures

Qamiu or variant - Ancient Egyptians-people of the black land.

---

i"Nubia," *Microsoft® Encarta® Africana.* © 1999 Microsoft Corporation. All rights reserved.

Ancient Ethiopia (present day Sudan), Called Nubia or Kash by the Ancient Egyptians, As the Source of Great Cultures in Ancient Times

The ancient historian Stephanus of Byzantium said:

"Ethiopia was the first established country on earth; and the Ethiopians were the first who introduced the worship of the gods, and who established laws."

The ancient historian Diodorus recorded the tradition of how the first Ethiopian/Nubian king Asar (Osiris) led a group of colonists up the Nile River and settled the area of the north-eastern corner of Africa which would later be known as "Kamit (Egypt)."

"From Ethiopia, he (Osiris) passed through Arabia, bordering upon the Red Sea to as far as India, and the remotest inhabited coasts; he built likewise many cities in India, one of which he called Nysa, willing to have remembrance of that (Nysa) in Egypt where he was brought up. At this Nysa in India he planted Ivy, which continues to grow there, but nowhere else in India or around it. He left likewise many other marks of his being in those parts, by which the latter inhabitants are induced, and do affirm, that this God was born in India. He likewise addicted himself to the hunting of elephants, and took care to have statues of himself in every place, as lasting monuments of his expedition."
             -Recorded by *Diodorus* (Greek historian 100 B.C.)

Thus we are to understand that the ancient Nubians colonized (settled) the area north of the sources of the Nile River as they followed its flow, looking for more fertile lands. Further, we learn, from the legend of Asar48, that after establishing civilization in Egypt, he proceeded to travel the ancient world and assisted those people in establishing civilizations outside of Africa, namely Asia Minor, India, China and southern Europe. Modern archeology has revealed that Asarian artifacts have been found in areas south of Uganda, specifically Zaire. Also, the Dogon peoples of West Africa hold that they are direct descendants of the Ancient Egyptians. So the influence of Asar (Ancient Egyptian civilization) was felt not only on the African continent, but far and wide. This is again supported by the ancient Greek and Roman historians.

"And upon his return to Greece, they gathered around and asked, "tell us about this great land of the Blacks called Ethiopia." And Herodotus said, "There are two great Ethiopian nations, one in Sind (India) and the other in Egypt."
             —Diodorus quoting Herodotus (c. 484-425 B.C.E.)

"India taken as a whole, beginning from the north and embracing what of it is subject to Persia, is a continuation of Egypt and the Ethiopians."
                                        -The Itinerarium Alexandri (A.C.E. 345)

Following the tradition as outlined above and taking into account the findings by geneticists and anthropologists which all show that human beings emerged from Africa through the Arabian desert and populated Asia, we are to understand that the Nubians gave rise to the Ancient Egyptians and the Ancient Egyptians gave rise to the peoples of Asia Minor and India.

Indians
↑
Colchians
↑
Egyptians
↑
Nubians (Ethiopians)

Colchis, Mesopotamia and Ancient Egypt in the First Millennium B.C.E.

The following excerpt comes from the "History" of Herodotus:

> There can be no doubt that the Colchians are an Egyptian race. Before I heard any mention of the fact from others, I had remarked it myself. After the thought had struck me, I made inquiries on the subject both in Colchis and in Egypt, and I found that the Colchians had a more distinct recollection of the Egyptians, than the Egyptians had of them. Still the Egyptians said that they believed the Colchians to be descended from the army of Sesostris. My own conjectures were founded, first, on the fact that they are black-skinned and have woolly hair, which certainly amounts to but little, since several other nations are so too; but further and more especially, on the circumstance that the Colchians, the Egyptians, and the Ethiopians, are the only nations who have practiced circumcision from the earliest times. The Phoenicians and the Syrians of Palestine themselves confess that they learnt the custom of the Egyptians; and the Syrians who dwell about the rivers Thermodon and Parthenius, as well as their neighbors the Macronians, say that they have recently adopted it from the Colchians. Now these are the only nations who use circumcision, and it is plain that they all imitate herein the Egyptians. With respect to the Ethiopians, indeed, I cannot decide whether they learnt the practice of the Egyptians, or the Egyptians of them- it is undoubtedly of very ancient date in Ethiopia- but that the others derived their knowledge of it from Egypt is clear to me from the fact that the Phoenicians, when they come to have commerce with the Greeks, cease to follow the Egyptians in this custom, and allow their children to remain uncircumcised. I will add a further proof to the identity of the Egyptians and the Colchians. These two nations weave their linen in exactly the same way, and this is a way entirely unknown to the rest of the world; they also in their whole mode of life and in their language resemble one another.

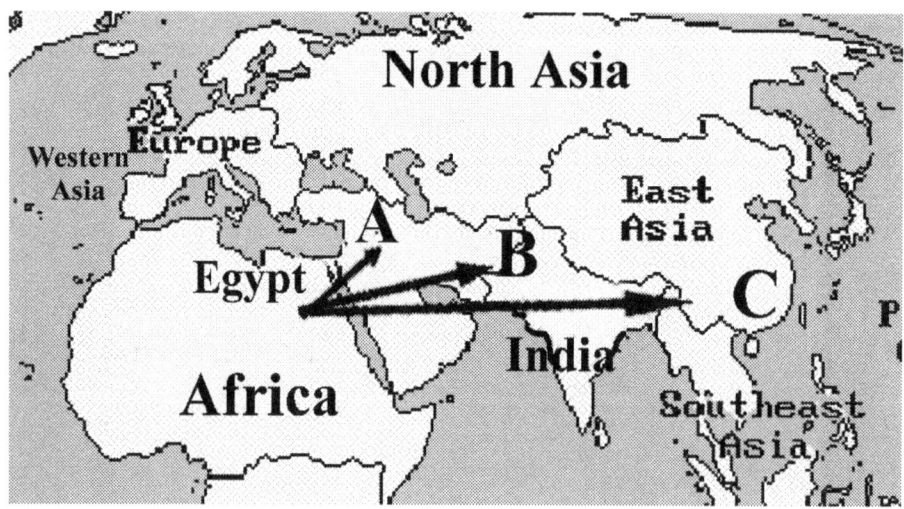

Above: Map of North Africa and Asia. A- Mesopotamia, B- Indus Valley, C- China

Colchis was an ancient country located on the eastern shore of the Black Sea. It was south of the Caucasus Mountains which are now part of the Republic of Georgia. Colchis was an independent nation until about 100 B.C.E., when it was conquered by Mithradates VI Eupator, king of Pontus. In Greek mythology, Colchis was the home of the princess Medea and the repository of the golden fleece sought by Jason and his Argonauts. The above excerpt shows that the peoples of Syria and northeastern Palestine (Caucasus – where the modern term Caucasian comes from) were originally Egyptians (dark skinned African peoples) who were strongly influenced by the culture of Egypt, not just through casual association, but by blood relation, being of the same skin color, practicing some of the same customs (including circumcision which the Jews adopted) and having similar language.

"Egyptians settled Ethiopia and Colchis."

-*Geography,* Strabo c. 64 B.C.E.,
(Greek historian and geographer)

Herodotus informed us in his writings that even the Colchians appear to be related to the Egyptians because of their customs and physical appearance, being "black skinned."

Ancient Egyptian Origin of the Chaldaens

The biblical name, "Ur of the Chaldees," refers to the Chaldaens, who settled in the area of southern Iraq about 900 B.C.E. The Book of Genesis (see 11:27-32) describes Ur as the starting point of the westward migration of the family of Abraham to Palestine about 1900-1800 B.C.E. Thus, at the time when Abraham would have lived, the Egyptian civilization was at the end of the Middle Kingdom Period (or Middle Empire 2,040-1,640 B.C.E.). Pharaoh Senusert I (Sesostris I), who reigned c. 1971-1928 B.C.E., built fortresses throughout Nubia and established trade with foreign lands; his rule stretched to the far east. He sent governors to Palestine. In more ancient times (12,000 B.C.E.), according to the Egyptian story of Asar (Osiris), the Egyptians ruled all of Asia Minor as far as India and beyond. Due to invasions and wars these lands were ceded to the conquering peoples. But during the Middle Kingdom Period, Palestine was once again controlled by Egypt as it was in ancient times.

The following are museum exhibits, which show the connection between Ancient Egypt and the peoples in Asia Minor in prehistoric times. These support the contention that Ancient Egyptian culture and religion were present in and strongly influenced Mesopotamian civilizations, including the Neo Assyrian and Sumerian.

Descriptions of the Nubians (Ethiopians) by the Ancient Greeks

We are given to understand by the testimony of the Ancient Egyptians themselves that their ancestors came from Nubia. These were the people referred to by the Greeks as Ethiopians. The term Ethiopians means "land of the burnt (black) faces."

Herodotus called them "The tallest, most beautiful and long-lived of the human races."

Homer referred to them as "The most just of men; the favorites of the gods."

Descriptions of the Ancient Egyptians and Nubians (Ethiopians) by the Ancient Greeks

"Still the Egyptians said that they believed the Colchians to be descended from the army of Sesostris. My own conjectures were founded, first, on the fact that they are black-skinned and have woolly hair."
　　　　　　　　　　　　　-History of Herodotus (Greek historian 484 B.C.E.)

"Egyptians settled Ethiopia and Colchis."
　　　　　　　　　-Geography, Strabo c. 64 B.C.E., (Greek historian and geographer)

"I shall speak of the king who reigned next, whose name was Sesostris[49] He, the priests said, first of all proceeded in a fleet of ships of war from the Arabian gulf along the shores of the Indian ocean, subduing the nations as he went, until he finally reached a sea which could not be navigated by reason of the shoals. Hence he returned to Egypt, where, they told me, he collected a vast armament, and made a progress by land across the continent, conquering every people which fell in his way.

In this way he traversed the whole continent of Asia, whence he passed on into Europe, and made himself master of Scythia and of Thrace, beyond which countries I do not think that his army extended its march."
　　　　　　　　　　　- History of Herodotus (Greek historian 484 B.C.E.)

"All the Indian tribes I mentioned ... their skins are all of the same color, much like the Ethiopians."
　　　　　　　　　　　　　-History of Herodotus (Greek historian 484 B.C.E.)

"And upon his return to Greece, they gathered around and asked, "tell us about this great land of the Blacks called Ethiopia." And Herodotus said, "There are two great Ethiopian nations, one in Sind (India) and the other in Egypt."
　　　　　　　　　　　　　　-Diodorus (Greek historian 100 B.C.)

"From Ethiopia, he (Osiris {Asar})[50] passed through Arabia, bordering upon the Red Sea to as far as India, and the remotest inhabited coasts; he built likewise many cities in India, one of which he called Nysa, willing to have remembrance of that (Nysa) in Egypt where he was brought up. At this Nysa in India he planted Ivy, which continues to grow there, but nowhere else in India or around it. He left likewise many other marks of his being in those parts, by which the latter inhabitants are induced, and do affirm, that this God was born in India. He likewise addicted himself to the hunting of elephants, and took care to have statues of himself in every place, as lasting monuments of his expedition."
　　　　　　　　　　　　　- Diodorus (Greek historian 100 B.C.)

Evidence of Contact-Eye Witness Accounts, Anthropology, Linguistics, Mythology

Asar (Osiris), the Avatar (Divine Incarnation) of Ancient Egypt, and founding King of Ancient Egypt (c. 12,000 B.C.E.) establishes civilization and religion in Asia and Europe.

"From Ethiopia, he (Osiris) passed through Arabia, bordering upon the Red Sea to as far as India, and the remotest inhabited coasts; he built likewise many cities in India, one of which he called Nysa, willing to have remembrance of that (Nysa) in Egypt where he was brought up. At this Nysa in India he planted Ivy, which continues to grow there, but nowhere else in India or around it. He left likewise many other marks of his being in those parts, by which the <u>latter inhabitants are induced, and do affirm, that this God was born in India.</u> He likewise addicted himself to the hunting of elephants, and took care to have statues of himself in every place, as lasting monuments of his expedition."

-Recorded by *Diodorus* (Greek historian 100 B.C.)

Figure: The Travels of Asar (Osiris) in Ancient Times

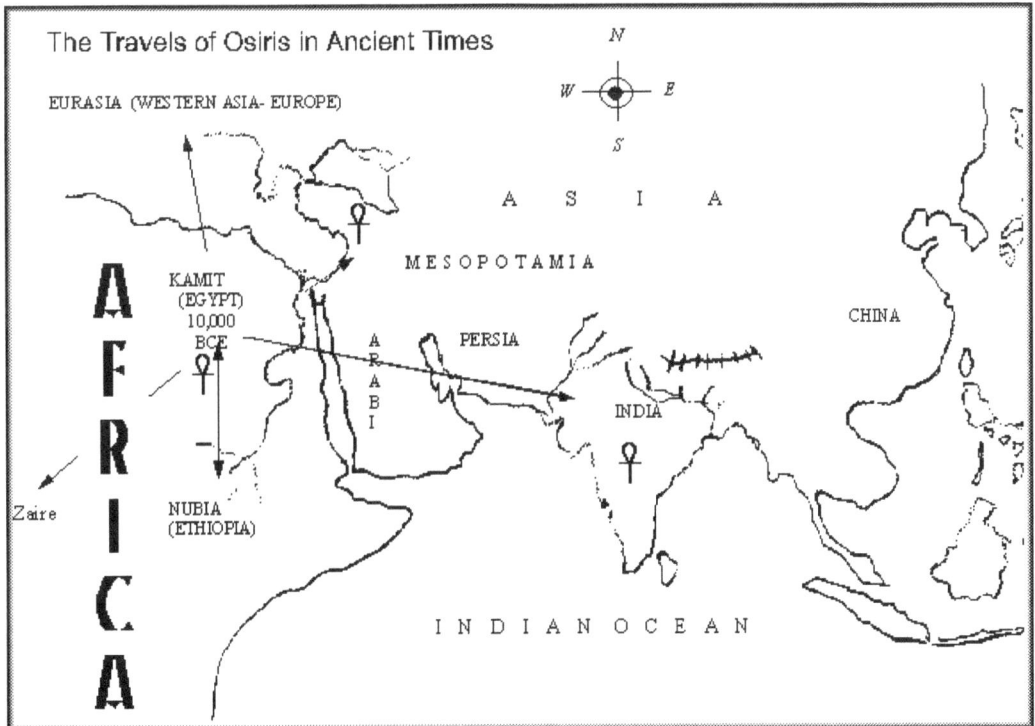

Above: A map of North-east Africa, Asia Minor and India, showing the three main locations of the use of the Ancient Egyptian Ankh symbol and also the geographic area where Asar (Osiris) traveled and spread the teachings of mystical spirituality which later became associated with Christianity in the Middle East, Rome and Greece, and Vedanta - Yoga in India.

In Support of the statements of Herodotus, Diodorus says the following:

"There are Egyptian columns as far off as NYASA, Arabia...Isis and Osiris led an army <u>into India, to the source of the Ganges, and as far as the Indus Ocean.</u>"

-Diodorus (Greek historian 100 B. C.)

King Senusert I {above} (Greek name: Sesostris) Controls the area from India to Europe in 1,971 B.C.E.

I shall speak of the king who reigned next, whose name was Sesostris. He, the priests said, first of all proceeded in a fleet of ships of war <u>from the Arabian gulf along the shores of the Indian ocean,</u> subduing the nations as he went, until he finally reached a sea which could not be navigated by reason of the shoals. Hence he returned to Egypt, where, they told me, he collected a vast armament, and made a progress by land across the continent, conquering every people which fell in his way.

In this way he traversed the whole continent of Asia, whence he passed on into Europe, and made himself master of Scythia and of Thrace,[i] beyond which countries I do not think that his army extended its march. For thus far the pillars which he erected are still visible, but in the remoter regions they are no longer

---

[i] **Scythia**, name given by the ancient Greeks after about 800BC to the homeland of the Scythians in the southeast part of Europe, eastward from the Carpathian Mountains to the Don River. **Thrace** (Latin *Thracia,* from Greek *Thraki*), region in southeast Europe, forming part of present-day Greece, Bulgaria, and Turkey. "Scythia," "Thrace," *Microsoft® Encarta® Encyclopedia 2000.* © 1993-1999 Microsoft Corporation. All rights reserved.

found. Returning to Egypt from Thrace, he came, on his way, to the banks of the river Phasis. Here I cannot say with any certainty what took place. Either he of his own accord detached a body of troops from his main army and left them to colonize the country, or else a certain number of his soldiers, wearied with their long wanderings, deserted, and established themselves on the banks of this stream.

- History of Herodotus (Greek historian 484 B.C.E.)[51]

The Ancient Egyptians were a colony of Ethiopians

"They also say that the Egyptians are colonists sent out by the Ethiopians, Osiris (Asar) having been the leader of the colony. For, speaking generally, what is now Egypt, they maintain, was not land, but sea, when in the beginning the universe was being formed; afterwards, however, as the Nile during the times of its inundation carried down the mud from Ethiopia, land was gradually built up from the deposit...And the larger parts of the customs of the Egyptians are, they hold, Ethiopian, the colonists still preserving their ancient manners. For instance, the belief that their kings are Gods, the very special attention which they pay to their burials, and many other matters of a similar nature, are Ethiopian practices, while the shapes of their statues and the forms of their letters are Ethiopian; for of the two kinds of writing which the Egyptians have, that which is known as popular (demotic) is learned by everyone, while that which is called sacred (hieratic), is understood only by the priests of the Egyptians, who learnt it from their Fathers as one of the things which are not divulged, but among the Ethiopians, everyone uses these forms of letters. Furthermore, the orders of the priests, they maintain, have much the same position among both peoples; for all are clean who are engaged in the service of the gods, keeping themselves shaven, like the Ethiopian priests, and having the same dress and form of staff, which is shaped like a plough and is carried by their kings who wear high felt hats which end in a knob in the top and are circled by the serpents which they call asps; and this symbol appears to carry the thought that it will be the lot of those who shall dare to attack the king to encounter death-carrying stings. Many other things are told by them concerning their own antiquity and the colony which they sent out that became the Egyptians, but about this there is no special need of our writing anything."

-Recorded by *Diodorus* (Greek historian 100 B.C.)

According to the Greek Classical Writers, The Inhabitants from the land area from Libya to Ethiopia are indigenous to the country. The Phoenicians and the Greeks are immigrants (foreigners) in the time of Herodotus.

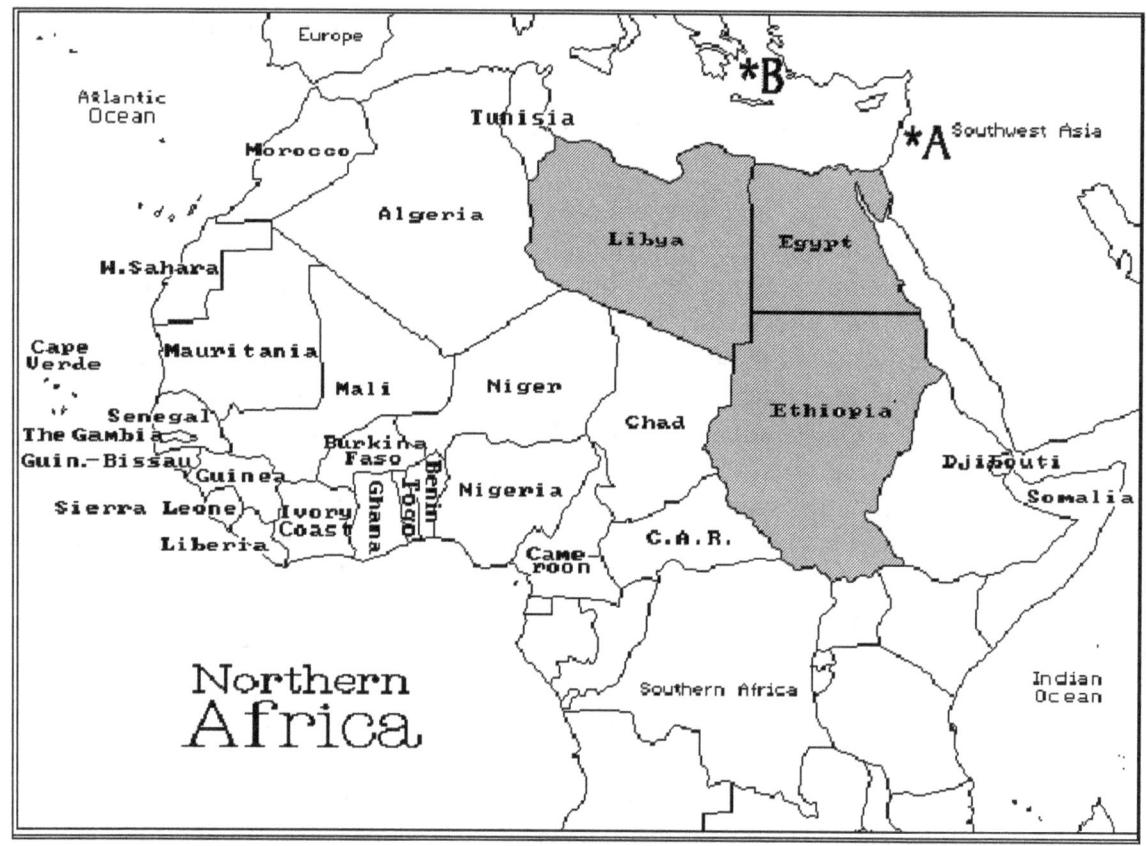

Map of northeast Africa showing Libya, Egypt and Ethiopia in the shaded area and (A) Phoenicia and (B) Greece.

The two indigenous are the Libyans and Ethiopians, who dwell respectively in the north and the south of Libya. The Phoenicians and the Greek are in-comers.
-History of Herodotus (Greek historian 484 B.C.E.)[52]

"Now the Ethiopians, as historians relate, were the first of all men and the proofs of this statement, they say, are manifest. For that they did not come into their land as immigrants from abroad but were the natives of it and so justly bear the name of autochthones (sprung from the soil itself), is, they maintain, conceded by practically all men..."

-Diodorus Siculus (Greek Historian)
writes in the time of Augustus (first century B.C.)

North Africa has experienced migrations from Asia and Europe since ancient times. Anthropologists and archaeologists have traced the routes of many prehistoric migrations by the current persistence of such effects. Blond physical characteristics among some of the Berbers of North Africa are thought to be evidence of an early Nordic invasion.[53] The term "Berber" refers to a people of n. Africa which includes Kabyle, Siwans, Tibu, and Tuareg, who gave the name to the Barbary States: Algeria, Atlas Mountains, Mauritania, Middle East, Moors, Morocco, Sahara, Tunisia.[i]

On the Inhabitants of North-East Africa: The Ethiopians and Libyans look the same except the Eastern Ethiopians (South) have straight hair and the Libyan Ethiopians (Northern Ethiopians) have woolly hair.

"They differed in nothing from the other Ethiopians, save in their language, and the character of their hair. For the eastern Ethiopians have straight hair, while they of Libya are more woolly-haired than any other people in the world."
-History of Herodotus (Greek historian 484 B.C.E.)[54]

On the Ethnicity of the people of India and their relation to the Ethiopians

In the epic Greek work, *The Odyssey*, Homer writes that the Greek gods go to visit Ethiopia which is located in two locations at opposite ends of the world geographically. Based on the statements of the other Greek writers this can be interpreted to mean that there are Ethiopians in India (the east) as well as in Africa, which is west of India.

"Now Neptune had gone off to the Ethiopians, who are at the world's end, and lie in two halves, the one looking West and the other East."
-Homer *The Odyssey* (Book I)

All the Indian tribes I mentioned ... their skins are all of the same color, much like the Ethiopians.
-History of Herodotus (Greek historian 484 B.C.E.)[55]

The Statement by Herodotus in reference to the Ethiopian (Nubian) origins of the Ancient Egyptians and the relationship to India is supported by the Greek writer Diodorus.

"And upon his return to Greece, they gathered around and asked, "tell us about this great land of the Blacks called Ethiopia." And Herodotus said, "There are two great Ethiopian nations, one in Sind (India) and the other in Egypt."
-*Diodorus* (Greek historian 100 B.C.)

Lucian of Samosata (Λουκιανὸς Σαμοσατεύς, Latin, Lucianus; c. AD 120 - after 180) was a rhetorician and satirist, writing in the Greek language, noted for his witty and scoffing nature. He was born in Samosata (now inundated in a reservoir of eastern Turkey), in the former kingdom of Commagene, which had been absorbed by the Roman Empire and made part of the province of Syria, thus he referred to himself as a "Syrian" (Harmon).[ii]

---

[i] Excerpted from *Compton's Interactive Encyclopedia*. Copyright (c) 1994, 1995 Compton's NewMedia, Inc. All Rights Reserved
[ii] From Wikipedia Encyclopedia

A story was written by Lucian called *Philopseudes,* about a sacred scribe of Memphis and the misadventures of his hero Eucrates In the story the Greek meet an Ancient Egyptian priest, a sage who was described as:

> *-a very holy man, clean-shaven, always wore linen, highly intelligent, spoke rather bad Greek, tallish, snub nose, thick lips, and rather thin legs."*

The description of the nose and lips of the sage follows the descriptions of other Greek writers in that it portray an image of an African or African related personality. The date of Lucian's writing supports the notion that the Ancient Egyptians had African features at the time of his writing which were the same as those from previous times.

The picture below is a painted Limestone stela of chamberlain Amunemhat [12 Dynasty]

Below: Statue of a Nubian king in Sudan, maybe it is king Natakamani. The statue was found in Tabo on the isle of Argo.[i] This image and the one above demonstrate that the features that the ancient Greeks described which are today recognized as "black" African facial features.

The Roman Empire acknowledges India as a part of Egypt and Ethiopia in ancient times.

"India taken as a whole, beginning from the north and embracing what of it is subject to Persia, is a continuation of Egypt and the Ethiopians."
                                              -The Itinerarium Alexandri (A.C.E. 345)

The records above establish the ethnicity of the Ancient Ethiopians, Libyans, Egyptians and Indians. They confirm a multitude of images which can be seen in ancient sites from around Egypt as well as in the museums from around the world. They show that while Egypt was a multi-ethnic country in the latter periods, it was essentially an outgrowth of Nubian culture and civilization.

---
[i] From Wikipedia Encyclopedia

Below- A Painting of an Ancient Egyptian man-From the Tomb of Rameses III, Thebes, Egypt, Africa

The image above of an Ancient Egyptian man recalls the image of modern day Nubians as well as present day South Indians.[i] In ancient times the dark skinned inhabitants of India covered the entire country. However, due to incursions by the Greeks, Aryans, Arabs, British and others, the darker skinned population has been relegated to the south portion of the Indian subcontinent. Since we know what modern day Ethiopians look like and we have pictorial evidence of what the Ancient Egyptians (above) and Ethiopians looked like, we can extrapolate the ethnicity of the other groups. The ancient Libyans, Egyptians and Indians were all of African descent and this group included, in ancient times, dark skin peoples with either curly or straight hair. This testimony shows that even in the time of Herodotus, the Indians displayed the same skin color and different hair textures as the Africans.

The testimony of Herodotus and Diodorus as to the ethnicity of the Indians and their ethnic link to the Ethiopians and Egyptians is confirmed by the modern science of genetics, which has proven not only a common ancestor for all human beings, who, having arisen in Africa, separated at around 100,000 years ago (see map below), dispersing across the world, but also have shown a link between the Ancient Egyptians and the earliest Indian civilization, the Harappan culture. In the massive work, *The History and Geography of Human Genes*, by Luigi Luca Cavalli-Sforza, Paolo Menozzi, Alberto Piazza, 1994, containing over 14 years of genetic records for the world population, it was shown that human beings are all genetically related.

---

[i] Keep in mind that in pre-Vedic times the indigenous inhabitants of India from the south to the north were Nubian in appearance. However, due to the changes and invasions that India has endured since that time, the descendants of the people who once lived in the Indus area and north India were amalgamated with the new ethnic groups or moved to the south. So in the present, the people of darkest hue generally will be found in the south and no longer in the north. Therefore, the Dravidians who live in the present day southern part of India are in part descendants of the Ancient Indusians.

Assyrian Descriptions of the Ancient Egyptians and Nubians

LEFT: In the year 667 B.C.E. the Assyrians invaded Kamit, pushed out the Egyptian-Nubian army and captured the capital city of Waset (Thebes). On a relief in the palace of the Assyrian king Assurbanibal (669-635), there is depicted the battle in which the Assyrians defeated the army of Kamit. The Assyrians (men with long beards and conned hats) took prisoners which included Kamitans and Nubians as well as the spoils of the victory back to their homeland. In this relief the Nubian and Kamitan soldiers are pictured equally, meaning that they did not recognize a "racial" difference, only the ethnic difference. As far as the physical appearance of the Nubians and Kamitans the Assyrians pictured them as having the same completion. Thus, here we have independent corroboration from the ancient Assyrians as to the ethnic homogeny of the Nubians and Kamitans.

Ancient Egyptian Depictions of Greek Pharaohs

Below: Philip Arrhidaeus, successor of Alexander, a Greek, in depicted in Red in accordance with Ancient Egyptian Iconographical standards to denote "Egyptian." Phillip was not an Egyptian by birth but by conquest and dictatorship. So he wanted the people to think of him as an Egyptian King and the practice was to depict Egyptians as red. However, otherwise we have seen Asiatics and others depicted as pale ("white). This means that the red color is not to denote a race or the color of the actual people but to demonstrate or differentiate one group of people from another for information purposes and not for segregation in the modern sense of Western Racism. (from the Napoleonic Expedition)

Ancient Egyptian Depictions of Egyptians (themselves) and Nubians

One reason for the confusion about the ethnicity of the Ancient Egyptians is the misunderstanding about their depictions of themselves. The men were represented in their art in two distinct forms, the red or reddish-brown and the black, both of which are used interchangeably. This is what the early Egyptologists such as Champollion witnessed before the colors on many depictions had been damaged or lost. In recent times, Western Egyptologists have mistakenly or intentionally characterized these images as evidence of ethnic or "racial" difference between the Ancient Egyptians and Nubians. However, the images from the Tombs of Rameses III and Seti I provide insight into this matter.

Below: Ancient Egyptians and Nubians depicted in the Tomb of Rameses III

 *Rtji* Ancient Egyptian    *Ahsu* Ancient Nubian

The Tomb of Seti I (1306-1290 B.C.E.-below) **which comes earlier** than that of Rameses III (above) shows a different depiction. Note that the same labels are used to describe the Egyptians and Nubians in the pictures of both tombs. So if the later picture uses the Nubian type (B) of image to describe the Egyptians that might tend to be regarded as meaning that the Egyptian type (A) was there first and the Nubian came later. Yet we have evidences of the Nubian type (B) both before and after the Egyptian type (B).

Below Ancient Egyptians and Nubians depicted in the Tomb of Seti I. Notice the similarity between the Nubian depiction below and the depictions from the Tomb of Huy (above).

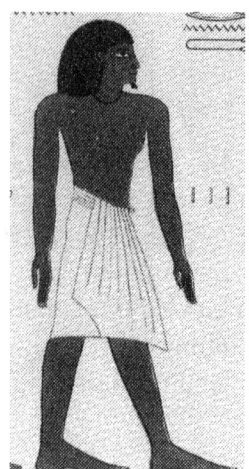
Rtji Ancient Egyptian (A)

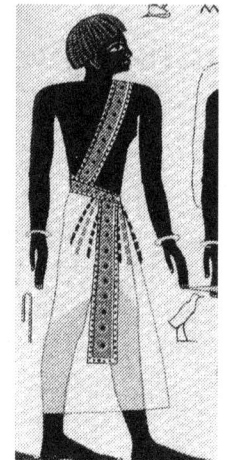
Ahsu Ancient Nubian (B)

There are two more depictions from Ancient Egypt, which shed light on the ethnological iconography of the Ancient Egyptians. First is an image from the temple of Rameses II at Abu Simbel. It provides us with the key to understanding the Kamitan depictions. At a time when Egypt and Nubia are competing with each other, Rameses symbolically brings tied up Nubian prisoners as offerings to Amun (See below).

Below left – late 20th century Nubian man. Below right-Nubian Prisoners of Rameses II -Image at the Abu Simbel Temple

Below-Ancient Egyptians (musicians) and Nubians (dancers) depicted in the Tombs of the Nobles with the same hue and features.

This image is important because it depicts the Nubian dancing girls as having the same hue as the Egyptian musician ladies. Therefore we may conclude that there was no difference in "racial" terms.

Below- Nubian King Taharka and the Queen offering to Amun (blue) and Mut (colored in yellow) depicted as a red Egyptians. 7th cent BCE

This picture is important because it depicts the Nubian Pharaoh of Egypt as a "red" man and we know from other naturalistic depictions that the Nubians were "black" Africans. So that means that this and other similar depictions are stylistic or ritualized and not meant to depict real life. There were no "red" men in Ancient Egypt; otherwise we would need to say that the Nubians and Greeks were red also because their Pharaohs were depicted in red.

Below-left, Egyptian man and woman-(tomb of Payry) 18th Dynasty displaying the naturalistic style (as people really appeared in ancient times) with dark brown sking done.. Below right- Egyptian man and woman-Theban tomb – depicted in the colors red and yellow, respectively.

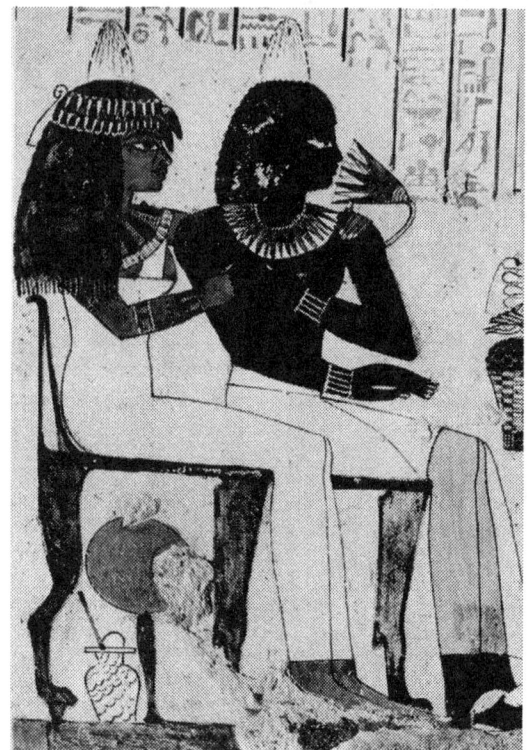

Below-left, Stele of Niptah - end of Middle Kingdom (man in red, woman in white).

Nubians (three figures prostrating) and Egyptians (standing figures) are depicted with the same colors of their skin of alternating black and brown -Tomb of Huy

Below: Nubians and Egyptians are depicted with the same colors of alternating black and brown -Tomb of Huy (image from drawing of 19th century explorers)

    The two pictures above are extremely important to our understanding of the ethnicity of the Ancient Egyptians, Nubians and Ethiopians. It is a rendition by French orientalist and architect *Prisse d' Avennes* (1807-1879 A.C.E.). It is understood by orthodox Egyptologists to be the procession of Nubians who are bringing gifts of gold to Huy, the viceroy of Kush, for the Egyptian king Tutankhamun (1333 B.C.E-1323 B.C.E). Note that the classic style of depicting Nubians with black or brown skin and the pronounced cheek line (scarification -see example right) as well as the feather on the head is maintained. In the same view, there are five figures standing behind the ones that are prostrating, who do not have the feathers or cheek lines, but do have the same skin tone and is represented in the classical style of depicting the Ancient Egyptians. Notice here that the depictions of the skin coloration of the Ancient Egyptians are the same as used for the Nubians (brown and black). While Ancient Egyptians and Nubians are depicted individually in brown and black color, the alternating pattern of brown and black is also used to more easily differentiate individuals when people are depicted in close proximity.

Above right - Nubian depictions from Akhnaton period (1352 B.C.E-1347 B.C.E) Brooklyn Museum (Photo by M. Ashby)

From the Tomb of Rameses III: The four branches of mankind, according to the Egyptians: A- Egyptian as seen by himself, B- Indo-European, C- Other Africans, D- Semites (Middle Easterners) (1194-1163 B.C.E.). [56]

Careful to avoid any future such exchanges which might prove to be more injurious to the orthodox Egyptological dogma, Diop was refused further access to materials or monuments for detailed research. However, by that time the injury to the orthodox Egyptological position had been done. Since that time other evidences, such as those presented in this book and by other scholars, have steadily chipped away at the orthodox Egyptological dogmas. In this sense the struggle[i] over the "guardianship," or as some might consider "ownership," over the prestige that comes with being able to consider oneself as an Ancient Egyptian Scholar will continue, because this is apparently a war of information in which western countries have taken the lead.

All kinds of information are valued, but the information on the origins of humanity and the metaphysics of spiritual evolution are both feared and awed by most ordinary human beings, and perhaps particularly the orthodox Egyptologists, because this information truly changes everything, from the concept of human origins to what is life all about. It brings the whole Western paradigm under scrutiny. Reflect on what would happen if those people in positions of authority as well as lay people in religions, governments and schools were suddenly faced with the realization that their knowledge is deficient, and ordinary people begin to understand that they are higher beings who should not be taken advantage of. This is the power of understanding the glory and truth about Ancient Egypt. All humanity, not just Africans or Europeans, can be

---

[i] over the ownership of the prestige of being a scholar of Egyptology.

transformed through it, for the better, to bring about a world culture based on unity camaraderie. The illusion which orthodox Egyptologists have promoted, and with which they have self-hypnotized themselves, will gradually give way to the truth, or else they will be left behind just as the Model "T" left the horse drawn buggy behind and, electricity left oil lamps behind.

The renowned Africologist, Basil Davidson, presented Dr. Diop briefly in Davidson's documentary program "Africa." He commented on this ancient ethnography and remarked that it was "rare," dismissing it as an anomaly. However, the following picture of an Ancient Egyptian "ethnography" was discovered by Dr. Muata Ashby in the book *Arts and Crafts of Ancient Egypt,* by Flinders Petrie. However, it was not ascribed as an ethnography, which included Ancient Egyptians, but rather, unknown "Abyssinians."

Above: Ancient Egyptian Depiction of Ethnic Groups (New Kingdom Dynastic Period)[57]
(Originally in the tomb of *Ramose* – drawn by Prisse d' Avennes)

The picture above is an Ancient Egyptian depiction of the four ethnic groups of the ancient world. Described by Petrie as "the Four Races" the picture is one of the ethnographies that have come down to us from Ancient Egypt. It should be noted that the formal ethnographies are rare but depictions showing the Nubians and Egyptians as having the same skin coloration are indeed quite abundant. Petrie describes the face to the far left as being a "Negro" (native African man). The next, from left to right, as a "Syrian" man, the third is described as an "Abyssinian," and the last as a "Libyan." In following along with this description by Petrie without having further insight into these classes of Ancient Egyptian art, it may go unnoticed that there is supposed to be an Ancient Egyptian person present. Having assigned the other "races," (i.e. Syrian, Libyan, Abyssinian), the Egyptian person has been omitted in the description of the group. This picture is a variation of the previous picture discovered by Dr. Diop. If the picture is rendered as the original, it would mean that the first man on the left that Petrie is referring to as a "Negro" is actually an Ancient Egyptian man, and the other person of African descent, labeled as an

"Abyssinian" man, would be the Nubian (Ethiopian), since the practice of scarification, common to Nubia, is rare or unknown in Ancient Egypt.

The term "Abyssinian" refers to languages often distinguished as belonging to the subgroup of Hamitic languages. The words Semitic (Asia Minor) and Hamitic (African) are derived from the names of Noah's sons, Shem and Ham (Christian Bible-Gen. 10). Ethiopia, formerly Abyssinia, is a republic in eastern Africa, currently bounded on the northeast by Eritrea and Djibouti, on the east and southeast by Somalia, on the southwest by Kenya, and on the west and northwest by Sudan. In ancient times the country was bounded in the north by Ancient Egypt. In ancient times Ethiopia and Egypt were strongly related. In fact, Ethiopia was the birthplace of the early Egyptians and also, according to Herodotus, the Indians as well. They appeared the same to him at the time of his travels through those countries. Thus, the picture shows that the Ancient Egyptians looked no different from other Africans.

Herodotus

"And upon his return to Greece, they gathered around and asked, "tell us about this great land of the Blacks called Ethiopia." And Herodotus said, "There are two great Ethiopian nations, one in Sind (India) and the other in Egypt."
—Herodotus (c. 484-425 BC)

It is unfortunate that as a result of the mishandling of the monuments due to destruction and neglect by the Arab peoples, the harsh elements and chemicals in the environment, the dams on the Nile River, and the push for tourism, many of the images that he saw can no longer be seen today in their original form, except for a limited amount of originals, like the one discovered by Dr. Diop. Very few monuments and images retain their original color so the only other means currently available to view the images in their original forms are from drawings or pictures made by the early Egyptologists during their expeditions to Egypt. However, we have sufficient images and corroborating texts to say with certainty that the ethnicity of the original peoples who created the culture and civilization of the Nile Valley (Ancient Egypt) were the same in appearance as those people living in modern day Nubia, i.e. they were indeed "black" Africans.

Images created by early Arab and European Explorers of the Ancient Egyptian Great Sphinx

The Great Sphinx is the oldest icon of Ancient Egypt that reveals the Ancient Egyptian religion as well as the physiognomy of the Ancient Egyptians. The Great Sphinx comes from the earliest known period of Ancient Egyptian culture, the predynastic era, from which the well known Dynastic period had its beginning, dating to 7,000-10,000 B.C.E.. Prior to the advent of photography, explorers used drawings to convey visual imagery. The images by Arab and explorers before the rise of European cultures and the images presented by European explorers, once the European nations had taken control of Egypt, display African features on the face of the Sphinx.

In the book *Serpent In the Sky*, the author, John Anthony West, commissioned a sketch artist from the New York City police department to do a study on the facial features of the Sphinx (especially the cheeks, lips and protruding lower physiognomy). He concluded that the facial features are clearly and unmistakably of a person of African descent and not of an Asiatic or European person.

The following images were created by 19th century European explorers of Egypt as well as pre-19th century Arab explorers of Egypt.

The Great Sphinx, covered in sand - Drawing by early Arab explorers – From the book *Descriptions of Egypt*

Painting of the Great Sphinx while buried up to its neck, by Denon 19 century

Sphinx-African from History of Egypt-Samuel Sharp 1876

Photograph of the Sphinx while buried up to its neck – 19th Century.

Images of People in Ancient Egypt with "African Features" in the Ancient Period and the Late Period of Ancient Egyptian History

Above top: Sculpture of an Ancient Egyptian Official from Sakkara (Old Kingdom) Brooklyn Museum

Above Below: Kamitan-Kushitic sculpture, described by the Brooklyn Museum as "Black man." (Hellenistic period)

The images above demonstrate that people with African facial and hair features were present in Ancient Egypt from its early period to the end. This finding would tend to suggest that the images that are more prevalent in the late period, of Greeks and Romans, are so due to the control of the government and the economy, by the Greeks and Romans, which gave them the power and the financial capacity to have images of themselves made and distributed. However, there were no Greek or Roman images in the earlier period. Nevertheless, even though the conquering groups were able to gain that power, in the Late Period, there is still evidence that the indigenous Ancient Egyptians were in the past and remained African looking peoples up to the end of Ancient Egyptian history when the Greeks, Romans and later, the Arabs came into Egypt in sufficient numbers to displace the indigenous population sand change its social and ethnic character.

DNA, Race and Ethnicity

DNA is an abbreviation for "Deoxyribonucleic acid." It is a complex giant molecule that contains the information needed for every cell of a living creature to create its physical features (hair, skin, bones, eyes, legs, etc., as well as their texture, coloration, their efficient functioning, etc.). All of this is contained in a chemically coded form. The Life Force of the Soul or Spirit engenders the impetus in the DNA to function. This in turn leads to the creation of the physical aspect of all living beings (human beings, animals, insects, microorganisms, etc.).

The DNA is what determines if two living beings are compatible with each other for the purpose of mating and producing offspring. If they are not compatible, then they are considered to be different species. All human beings are compatible with each other therefore, they are members of a single species, i.e. one human race.

Figure 1: The Spread of Humanity.[58]

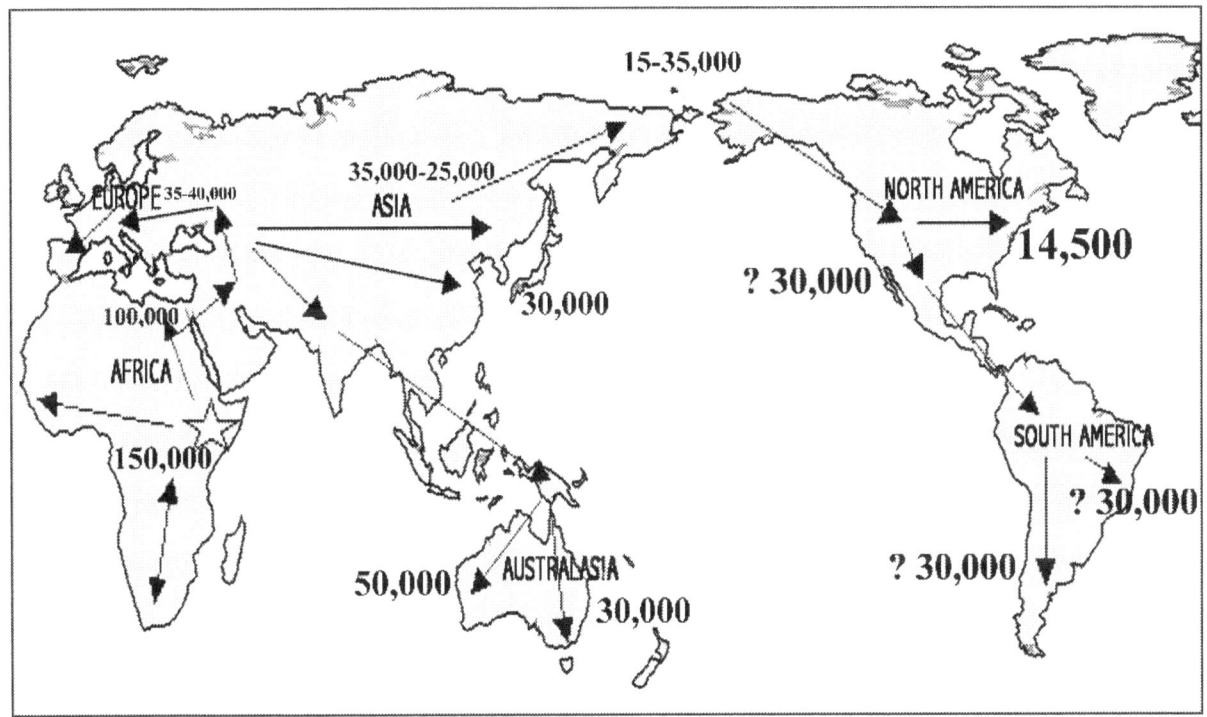

The map above shows the movement of humanity from its original origins in central equatorial Africa in 150,000 B.C.E. to the rest of the world. It has been demonstrated philosophically that the human body is only a vehicle of the spirit that is directed by its DNA. According to the spiritual philosophy of African Religion as well as Indian Religion, the soul has human experiences but it is not bound by them or comes into existence as a result of them. That is, DNA does not give rise to a soul. The soul associates with a body in order to have human experiences. Therefore, DNA is an instrument of the Spirit, which it uses to create the body and thereby avail itself of physical existence and experiences. According to mystical philosophy, the soul chooses the particular world, country, and family in which to incarnate in order to have the kind of experiences it wants to experience. This is all expressed in the physical plane through the miracle of DNA.[59]

Below: A drawing of a Human DNA strand.

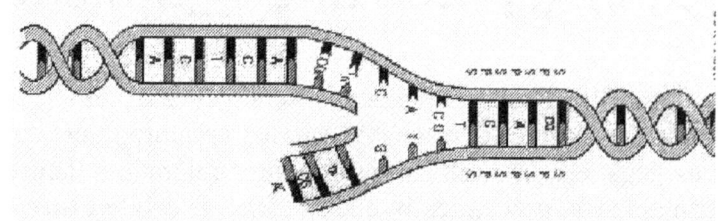

The ethnicity of the Ethiopians, Ancient Egyptians and Indians is not presented here to elevate the concept of race or one group over another, but to acknowledge ethnicity as one of the connection factors described in ancient times between these groups. When Herodotus and others wrote about the Ethiopians, Ancient Egyptians and Indians as being "black," they did not have the racial connotations that are applied in modern times in mind. In fact this term (race) is only used in this work in lieu of a better term devoid of the baggage of racism. Ethnicity is a better, though limited term that can be used. Since the concept of race, racial types and racism are false, then it follows that skin color is a cultural trait and not a racial trait. However, those of different ancestries may adopt the culture of those whose skin color trait is different and certain segments of modern society have attempted to misrepresent history, promoting the idea that people of African descent or ethnicity had little or no part in creating civilization. Thus, we must be clear when speaking about or using the skin color and clearly note that it is referenced only as a descriptive term for identifying cultural descent and ethnic genealogy. In later times (Late Period and early Christian Period), lighter skinned peoples (ethnic groups) migrated from Europe and Asia Minor to North-Eastern Africa, making it a multiethnic mixed society. It must be clearly understood that the notion of ethnicity (what in modern times some people refer to as "race") was known by the Ancient Egyptians, but the concepts of racism and racial bias were not known in ancient times. The terms race and racism are modern day misinterpretations of culture and ethnicity. The scientific community in general, and especially the science of genetics, does not recognize any such concept as it has been amply proven that all human beings belong to the same "race." Within this human race, human beings manifest variations due to geography, diet, beliefs, history and length of time (generations) removed from the original African ancestry, etc., and not due to genetics.[60] Therefore, the concept of race and its acute form, racism, are held by the ignorant. Since the concept of race is bogus, those who violently uphold the idea of race must be considered as psychologically impaired, since the belief in untruth in the face of truth must be recognized as a sign of mental illness. A primary task for all systems of spirituality is to dispel the misconceptions about race since this aspect of human interaction is a degrading force in civilization. It is a source of strife and suffering as well as misunderstanding of spiritual and religious teachings.

Finally, it was the Ancient Egyptians who first realized the underlying unity of all humanity which transcends physical manifestations. This conclusion is evident from the following passage of the Hymns to Aton in which Sage Akhnaton recites words of adoration and praise to the Divine Self (called Aton).

> Thou settest every person in his place.
> Thou providest their daily food, every man having the portion allotted to him;
> [thou] dost compute the duration of his life.
> Their tongues are different in speech, their characteristics (or forms), and likewise their skins (in color), giving distinguishing marks to the dwellers in foreign lands...
> Thou makest the life of all remote lands.
> —Akhnaton

Other Evidences

This book mainly presented historical, eyewitness testimony accounts from Greeks and Romans and others and self-depictions by the ancient Egyptians to demonstrate their African ancestry. Other evidences presented by other researchers includes:

Paleoanthropology: the study of Ancient Egyptian skeletons and skulls reveals similarity to the present day Black Nubian ethnic group as well as people of the Nilotic region (living along the interior of the Nile River) and East Africa.

Melanin: Cheikh Anta Diop, an African scientist, Egyptologist and historian invented a means to test the melanin levels in people's skin. After testing Ancient Egyptian mummies at the museum in Paris, France he found that they were consistent with melanin levels of black people.

Blood Types: After testing the blood type of modern Egyptians Diop found the "same group B as the populations of western Africa on the Atlantic seaboard and not the A2 Group characteristic of the white race prior to any crossbreeding" even after inter-mixture with foreign invaders such as Greeks, Romans, Assyrians, Arabs, etc.

Cultural compatibility: studies of Ancient Egyptian and other African cultures reveal commonalities not found between Ancient Egypt and European or Arab cultures such as in practices related to religious traditions, religious philosophy or the practice of totemism.

Language compatibility: Cheikh Anta Diop made an extensive study of African languages and found that the Ancient Egyptian language, the modern Coptic of Egypt (descendant of the Ancient Egyptian) and Wolof of West Africa are related. He determined that Coptic and Wolof originated in the Ancient Egyptian.

NOTES and REFERENCES

[1] Published in 1833 by the son of Champollion-Figeac, brother of Jean Fransçois Champollion.
[2] Ruins of Empires by Count Volney, (Diop, 1974, p. 28).
[3] The Zambesi and Its Tributaries, p. 526. N. Y., 1866.
[4] The Uganda Protectorate, Vol. II, p. 472. London, 1902.
[5] The Mediterranean Races, p. 243. N. Y., 1901.
[6] Royal Soc. of Arts Jour., Vol. XLIX, p. 594. 1901.
[7] *Egyptiene ancienne.* Paris: Collection l'Univers, 1839, pp 26-27
[8] Rawlinson, G. The Story of Egypt, p. 252. London. 1887.
[9] *Historie ancienne des peubles de l'Orient.*
[10] *Heresy in the University: The Black Athena Controversy and the Responsibilities of American Intellectuals* by Jacques Berlinerblan
[11] George, *Crimes of Perception,* xi (emphasis added); Peters, *Heresy and Authority,* 15, 17.
[12] P. L. Berger, Heretical Imperative, 28. Foucault, History *of* Sexuality, vol. 1, 93. On Foucault's use of this term, see James Miller, Passion *of* Michel Foucault, 108. Char, "Partage formel XXII," 0euvres completes, 160.
[13] Bernal, Black Athena 1: 2 (emphasis in original).
[14] Random House Encyclopedia Copyright (C) 1983,1990
[15] "Vergil," Microsoft (R) Encarta. Copyright (c) 1994
[16] *The Aeneid By Virgil*, Translated by John Dryden
[17] Troy (Asia Minor), also Ilium (ancient Ilion), famous city of Greek legend, on the northwestern corner of Asia Minor, in present-day Turkey. "Troy (Asia Minor)," Microsoft (R) Encarta. Copyright (c) 1994
[18] "Memnon," Microsoft (R) Encarta. Copyright (c) 1994
[19] Random House Encyclopedia Copyright (C) 1983,1990
[20] *The Complete Temples of Ancient Egypt*, Richard Wilkinson, (C) 2000
[21] Random House Encyclopedia Copyright (C) 1983,1990
[22] Metropolitan Museum New York
[23] Encarta Encyclopedia, Copyright (c) 1994
[24] Photo by Gakuji Tanaka
[25] Petrie Museum, London England.
[26] **The Middle Passage: White Ships Black Cargo** by Tom Feelings, John Henrik, Dr Clarke
[27] **Stolen Legacy**, George James
[28] *Black Athena, The Afroasiatic Origins of Classical Civilization* by Martin Bernal
[29] **Destruction of Black Civilization:** Great Issues of a Race from 4500bc to 2000ad by Chancellor Williams
[30] *Stolen Legacy,* George G.M. James
[31] *From Egypt to Greece,* M. Ashby C. M. Books 1997
[32] *Manetho,* W. G. Waddell
[33] Encarta Encyclopedia, Copyright (c) 1994
[34] Gen. 25:26
[35] Gen. 47:9
[36] 60+130+430=620.
[37] 400-130-60=210.
[38] *Bible Myth: The African Origins of the Jewish People* Gary Greenberg
[39] *The Power of Myth*, Joseph Campbell
[40] *Traveler's Key to Ancient Egypt*, John Anthony West
[41] *Black Man of The Nile and His Family* by
[42] *The African Origin of Civilization, Civilization or Barbarism,* Cheikh Anta Diop
[43] *Compton's Interactive Encyclopedia.* Copyright (c) 1994, 1995

[44] Copyright © 1995 Helicon Publishing Ltd Webster Encyclopedia
[45] *Gods and Symbols of Ancient Egypt* by Manfred Lurker
[46] *Compton's Interactive Encyclopedia*. Copyright (c) 1994, 1995
[47] *Compton's Interactive Encyclopedia*. Copyright (c) 1994, 1995
[48] See the book *Resurrecting Osiris* by Muata Ashby
[49] Senusert I, reigned in 1,971. B.C.E.
[50] Reigned c. 10,000 B.C.E.
[51] *The Histories,* Herodotus, Translated by Aubrey de Selincourt- *The History of Herodotus By Herodotus,* Translated by George Rawlinson
[52] *The Histories,* Herodotus, Translated by Aubrey de Selincourt- *The History of Herodotus By Herodotus,* Translated by George Rawlinson
[53] "Migration," Microsoft (R) Encarta. Copyright (c) 1994 Microsoft Corporation.
[54] *The Histories,* Herodotus, Translated by Aubrey de Selincourt- *The History of Herodotus By Herodotus,* Translated by George Rawlinson
[55] *The Histories,* Herodotus, Translated by Aubrey de Selincourt- *The History of Herodotus By Herodotus,* Translated by George Rawlinson
[56] Photo: From Cheikh Anta Diop's "Civilisation ou Barbarie", Courtesy of Présence Africaine.
[57] *Arts and Crafts of Ancient Egypt*, Flinders Petrie
[58] Image based on the findings contained in the books *The Great Human Diasporas,* Luigi Luca Cavalli-Sforza, Francesco Cavalli-Sforza. *The Cambridge Encyclopedia of Human Evolution,* Editor, Steve Jones
[59] Websters Encyclopedia 1996
[60] Encarta. Copyright (c) 1994 Funk & Wagnall's Corporation.

Index

Abdu 10
Abraham 13, 75
Abu Simbel 47, 88
Abyssinia 15, 94
Abyssinian 93, 94
Academia 64
Acts 63
Aeneid, The 24, 102
Africa.4, 7, 8, 12, 14, 15, 16, 19, 21, 22, 23, 25, 26, 34, 37, 67, 68, 71, 72, 73, 74, 77, 80, 81, 84, 93, 94, 99, 100, 101, 110, 114
African American 16, 23, 66
African Religion ... 99, 108, 111, 113
Ahsu 33, 87, 88
Akhenaton 23, 25, 27, 28
Akhnaton 10, 25, 27, 34, 92, 100, 103
Alexander the Great 17
Allopathic 108
Amenhotep III 23, 24, 25, 40
Amenta 111
Amentet 112
American Heritage Dictionary, Dictionary 5, 23, 26, 113
Americas 15
Amun 10, 47, 69, 88, 89
Amunhotep 23, 62
Amunmhat I 14, 23
Amun-Ra-Ptah 10
Ancient Egypt 2, 4, 5, 7, 8, 9, 10, 12, 14, 15, 16, 17, 18, 19, 20, 21, 22, 23, 24, 25, 26, 27, 33, 37, 47, 60, 61, 62, 63, 64, 65, 66, 67, 69, 71, 72, 73, 74, 75, 76, 77, 79, 81, 82, 84, 85, 86, 87, 88, 89, 91, 92, 93, 94, 95, 98, 100, 101, 102, 103, 108, 109, 110, 111, 112, 113, 114
Ancient Greeks 75, 76
Ancient Nubian 33, 87, 88
Ankh 77
Anu 10, 111
Anu (Greek Heliopolis) . 10, 111
Anunian Theology 111
Aquarian Gospel. 68, 72, 76, 77, 78
Arabia 68, 72, 76, 77, 78
Arabs 12, 16, 17, 21, 68, 84, 101
Aristotle 20
Aryan 109
Aryans 84
Asar ...10, 69, 72, 75, 76, 77, 79, 111, 112

Asar and Aset 111
Asarian Resurrection... 110, 112, 113
Aset 10, 109, 111, 112
Aset (Isis) 10, 109, 111, 112
Asia 4, 16, 22, 26, 63, 72, 73, 74, 75, 76, 77, 78, 80, 94, 100, 102
Asia XE "Asia" Minor 4
Asia Minor 16
Asia Minor 22
Asia Minor 26
Asia Minor 72
Asia Minor 73
Asia Minor 75
Asia Minor 75
Asia Minor 77
Asia Minor 94
Asia Minor 100
Asia Minor 102
Asiatic 4, 17, 26, 95
Assyrian 22, 75, 85
Assyrians 61, 85, 101
Astral 111
Astral Plane 111
Athena 18, 21, 102
Atlantis 114
Aton 10, 27, 28, 100
Augustus 12, 80
Avatar 77
Awakening 111
Babylon 25, 63
Baghdad 63
Barbarism 102
Being 18, 23, 112
Ben-jochannan, Yosef A. A. ...66
Berber 68, 80
Bernal, Martin 18, 102
Bible 4, 13, 21, 60, 62, 63, 67, 94, 102, 112
Black. 2, 4, 6, 16, 18, 21, 25, 26, 34, 69, 70, 71, 75, 98, 101, 102
Black Athena 18, 21, 102
Blackness 71
Black-skinned 74, 76
Blood 101
Book of Coming Forth By Day 111
Book of the Dead, see also Rau Nu Prt M Hru 111
Brazilians 16
Brooklyn Museum 26, 37, 92, 98
Buddha 114
Buddhism 10, 69, 111
Buddhist 110

Byzantine 12
Cairo 27, 44, 67, 68
Campbell, Joseph 102
Catholic 112
Catholic Church 112
Chaldaens 75
Chaldeans 75
Champollion, Jean Franșcois. 14, 15, 102
Champollion-Figeac 15, 16, 102
Child 67, 112
China 72, 74
Christ 17, 24, 111
Christianity 12, 22, 62, 66, 77, 108, 111, 112
Chronology 66
Church 19, 65, 112
Civility 23
Civilization 2, 4, 7, 12, 18, 19, 23, 102, 109
Clarke, John H. 66
Class, ruling class 17
Colchians 15, 73, 74, 75, 76
Colchis 74, 75, 76
colonialism 12
Color 29, 30, 33, 34, 69
Colossi of Memnon 24
Congress 2
Consciousness 111
Consciousness, human 108
Coptic 101, 111
Copts 15, 16, 18
cosmic force 112, 114
Creation 62, 69, 70, 110, 111
Culture...2, 4, 7, 22, 23, 60, 110, 114
Dark Ages 14
Darwin 62
Darwin, Charles 62
Davidson, Basil 93
December 112
Delta 8
Demotic 79
Denderah 10, 111
Devotional Love 110
Diaspora 16, 66
Diet 109
Diodorus.. 13, 19, 20, 25, 72, 76, 77, 78, 79, 80, 81, 84
Diop, Cheikh Anta..... 19, 66, 67, 68, 92, 93, 94, 101, 102, 103
DNA 99, 100
Dogon 72
Duat 111
Dynastic period 61, 95

Dynastic Period. 17, 34, 60, 61, 93
Edfu 10, 111
Egyptian Antiquities Organizations..................... 66
Egyptian Book of Coming Forth By Day............................ 111
Egyptian civilization. 15, 17, 63, 66, 72, 75
Egyptian Mysteries 109, 113
Egyptian Physics 111
Egyptian proverbs................ 110
Egyptian religion 19, 63, 95
Egyptian Yoga 108, 109, 110, 111
Egyptian Yoga see also Kamitan Yoga 108, 109, 110, 111
Egyptologists 12, 15, 17, 18, 23, 60, 61, 62, 64, 65, 66, 69, 87, 91, 92, 94, 113
Enlightenment..... 108, 109, 110, 111, 112, 113, 114
Eos 24
Ethics 4, 109
Ethiopia ...24, 25, 71, 72, 74, 75, 76, 77, 79, 80, 81, 83, 94
Ethiopian priests 79
Ethnic................................... 93
Ethnicity 4, 81, 99, 100
Ethnographies 22, 93
Eucharist 111
Euphrates River 63
Europe15, 16, 22, 23, 72, 76, 77, 78, 80, 100
European explorers 61, 95
Evil 113
Evolution, theory of............. 103
Exercise 111
Eye..................................... 77
Feelings 102
First Intermediate Period 12
Form 115
France 101, 103
Galla culture 15
Geb 111
Genealogy........................... 23
Genes 84
Genetic................................ 68
Geography 75, 76, 84
Ghandi, Mahatma 23
Giza 13
Giza Plateau........................ 13
God 63, 72, 76, 77, 109, 110, 111, 112, 114
Goddess 112
Goddesses 110, 113
Gods............. 79, 103, 110, 113
gods and goddesses24, 111, 113, 114

Gold 70, 71
Good 113
Gospels 112
Great Pyramid 13
Great Pyramids 13
Greece 18, 19, 24, 60, 72, 76, 77, 78, 80, 81, 94, 102, 109, 114
Greek classical writers 14, 17, 18, 20, 21, 25
Greek Classical writers 20
Greek philosophers 12, 23
Greek philosophy 108
Greeks 12, 16, 19, 20, 22, 23, 24, 74, 75, 76, 78, 80, 83, 84, 101
Greenberg, Gary............. 63, 102
Halif Terrace site................... 64
Ham................................ 60, 94
Hapi....................................... 8
Harappan culture 84
Hathor 111, 112, 113
Hatshepsut, Queen 26
Health.......................... 108, 111
Heart 112
Heart (also see Ab, mind, conscience)...................... 112
Heaven 112
Hebrew.................... 13, 21, 69
Hebrew Bible 21
Hebrews 63
Heliopolis.......................... 10
Hell 19
Heretical........................... 102
Herodotus 12, 15, 19, 20, 21, 25, 63, 72, 74, 75, 76, 78, 79, 80, 81, 84, 94, 100, 103
Heru 8, 10, 111, 112, 113
Heru (see Horus)8, 10, 111, 112, 113
Hetheru 10, 113
Hetheru (Hetheru, Hathor) 10, 113
Hetkaptah see also Menefer, Memphite 10
Hieroglyphic 110
Hieroglyphic Writing, language 110
Hilliard, Asa G. 67
Hinduism...................... 10, 111
Hindus 113
Homer 24, 75, 81
Howe, Steven 21
Humanity 99, 113
Hyksos 61, 67
Hymns to Aton 100
Image 47, 103
imperialism 64
India .. 10, 12, 19, 25, 34, 69, 72, 73, 75, 76, 77, 78, 81, 83, 84, 94, 109, 110

Indian Yoga 108, 109
Indus............34, 74, 78, 84, 109
Indus Valley 34, 74, 109
Initiate 109
Iraq 25, 75
Isfet...................................67
Isis 78, 109, 111, 112
Isis and Osiris, see Asar and Aset 78
Isis, See also Aset..78, 109, 111, 112
Islam 17, 22, 66, 108
Israel..............................63, 64
Jacob (and Israel) 63
Jamaica................................16
James, George G. M. 66
James, George G.M. 102
Japheth 60
Jesus 111, 112
Jesus Christ.........................111
Jewish........... 13, 20, 63, 69, 102
Jewish XE "Jewish" people ...63
Jews.....................13, 62, 63, 75
Joseph 13, 102
Joseph Campbell 102
Judaism.................12, 66, 108
Judeo-Christian 62
Kabbalah 108
Kaffirs 15, 16
Kamit...8, 10, 12, 17, 18, 26, 61, 67, 68, 69, 71, 72
Kamit (Egypt)..8, 10, 12, 17, 18, 26, 61, 67, 68, 69, 71, 72, 85, 113
Kamitan ...23, 26, 61, 62, 67, 68, 69, 71, 85, 88, 98, 109, 114
Karma................................110
Karnak...........................62, 65
Kemetic 62, 67, 68, 88, 114
Kenya.................................94
Khemn, see also ignorance ...113
King...12, 25, 27, 61, 77, 78, 86, 89, 112, 114
Kingdom.. 12, 17, 26, 75, 90, 93, 112
Kingdom of Heaven 112
KMT (Ancient Egypt). See also Kamit..............................67
Koran.................................63
Krishna..........................69, 112
Kush 71, 91
Latin 24, 78, 81
Lefkowitz, Mary....................19
Libya 15, 16, 80, 81
Libyans..... 12, 16, 80, 81, 83, 84
Life 62, 99, 110, 114
Life Force 99, 110
Linguistics 77
Love 110

Lower Egypt 8, 9
Luxor 26, 65
Maat 8, 23, 67, 110, 112, 114
MAAT 68, 110
MAATI 110
Manetho 12, 62, 102
Manetho, see also History of Manetho 12, 62, 102
Matter 70, 111
Meditation 109, 110
Mediterranean 8, 26, 63, 102
Medu Neter 113
Memnon 23, 24, 25, 102
Memphis 10, 82
Memphite Theology 111
Men-nefer, see also Het-Ka-Ptah, Memphis 10
Mesopotamia . 25, 60, 63, 67, 74
Metaphysics 111
Metropolitan Museum ... 34, 102
Middle Ages 14
Middle East 77, 81, 92, 108
Middle East XE "Middle East" erners 92
Middle Kingdom 12, 17, 26, 48, 75, 90
Middle Kingdom XE "Middle Kingdom" Period, Ancient Egypt 75
Min 111
Minoan 48
Moors 16, 81
Moses 13, 62, 63
Move, relocate 14
Muntuhotep 25, 26
Muslims 61
Mut 47, 89
Mysteries 109, 113
mystical philosophy 99
Mysticism ... 4, 69, 109, 111, 113
Mythology 77
Neberdjer 108
Negro race 15, 16, 18
Nehast 113
Net, goddess 10
Neter 10, 110, 111, 113
Neterian 113
Neteru 113
New Kingdom 12, 17, 93
Nile River ... 7, 8, 12, 72, 94, 101
Nile Valley 7, 8, 18, 94
Noah 60, 94
North East Africa . See also
   Egypt
   Ethiopia
      Cush 7
North East Africa. See also
   Egypt
   Ethiopia

Cush 7
Nubia. 14, 15, 23, 25, 26, 71, 72, 75, 88, 94
Nubian 12, 14, 17, 23, 25, 27, 33, 34, 35, 45, 47, 71, 72, 81, 83, 84, 85, 87, 88, 89, 92, 94, 101
Nubian King Taharka 47, 89
Nubian prisoners 88
Nubians 5, 14, 22, 25, 30, 33, 47, 72, 73, 75, 76, 84, 85, 87, 88, 89, 91, 93
Nut 111
Nysa 72, 76, 77
Obenga 67, 68
Ocean 78
Octavian 12
Old Kingdom 12, 26, 98
Orion Star Constellation 112
Orthodox . 22, 23, 64, 65, 66, 91, 92, 113
Osiris. 10, 72, 75, 76, 77, 78, 79, 103, 111, 113
Paleoanthropology 101
Palermo Stone 12
Palestine 62, 63, 74, 75
Papyrus of Turin 12
Passion 102
Per-aah 27, 69
Persia 73, 83
Persian Gulf 63
Persians 12, 61
PERT EM HERU, SEE ALSO BOOK OF THE DEAD ... 111
Petrie, Flinders ... 15, 17, 93, 103
Pharaoh ... 23, 25, 26, 27, 40, 61, 62, 69, 75
Phenotype 5
Philae 10, 111
Philosophy 2, 4, 8, 108, 109, 110, 111, 112, 114
Phoenicia 80
Physical 115
Plato 19, 20
Plutarch 20
pressure 65, 66
priests and priestesses .. 110, 113
Priests and Priestesses .. 109, 113
Psychology 111
Ptah 10, 111
Ptolemy, Greek ruler 12
Punt 68
Pyramid 10
Pyramid Texts 10
Pyramidiot 64
Pyramids 15, 19, 23
Pythagoras 20
Qamit 71
Queen 28, 47, 61, 89, 114
Ra 10, 110

Race 4, 14, 15, 17, 102
Racism 5, 86
Ramases 15
Rameses II 33, 35, 47, 62, 84, 87, 88, 92
Reality 19
Realization 109
Red 34, 36, 70, 72, 76, 77, 86
Red Sea 72, 76, 77
Religion. 2, 4, 99, 109, 111, 112, 113, 114
Renaissance 15
Resurrection . 110, 111, 112, 113
Ritual 113
Rituals 112
Roman 12, 22, 24, 25, 72, 81, 83
Roman XE "Roman" Empire.81
Roman Empire 24
Roman Empire 83
Romans 12, 23, 24, 101
Rome 12, 24, 77, 114
Rtji 33, 87, 88
Sages 108, 111, 112, 114
Sahara 81
Saints 111
Sais 10
Sakkara 10, 26, 98
Sargon I 63
Saudi Arabia 68
Schwaller de Lubicz 65
Sebai 114
Second Intermediate Period.... 12
See also Ra-Hrakti 10, 110
See Nat 10
Self (see Ba, soul, Spirit, Universal, Ba, Neter, Heru). 100, 109, 110, 111, 113
Sema 108, 114, 115
Semite 16
Semitic 63, 94
Senusert .. 25, 26, 44, 75, 78, 103
Senusert I 25, 26, 75, 78, 103
Serpent 65, 66, 95
Serpent in the Sky 65, 66
Set 113
Seti I 33, 87, 88, 110
Sex 15, 17, 111
Sexuality 102
Shabaka 17
Shedy 109
Shem 94
Shetaut Neter 10, 111, 113
Shetaut Neter See also Egyptian Religion 10, 111, 113
Shunya 69
Sirius 112
Sky 65, 66, 95
slavery 14, 113
Somaliland 68

Soul 99, 113
South India 84
Spain 16
Sphinx 10, 12, 13, 15, 57, 58, 95, 96, 97
Spirit 70, 99
Spiritual discipline 109
Spirituality 108, 109
Stele of Niptah 48, 90
Stele of Niptah, Minoan ... 48, 90
Stephanus of Byzantium 72
Strabo 19, 20, 75, 76
Study 67
Sublimation 111
Sudan 25, 45, 71, 72, 83, 94
Sumer 63
Sumerian 75
Supreme Being 112
Syria 25, 75, 81
Taharka 89
Tantra 111
Tantra Yoga 111
Taoism 108
Ta-Seti 23
Temple 47, 88, 111, 113
Temple of Aset 111
The Absolute 108
The Black 2, 4, 18, 102
The God 110
The Gods 110

The Illiad and The Odyssey ... 24
The Itinerarium Alexandri 73, 83
Theban Theology 108
Thebes 10, 84, 85, 108, 110
Theology 112
Time 65
time and space 69, 70, 113
Tithonus 24
Tomb. 31, 33, 35, 84, 87, 88, 91, 92, 110
Tomb of Huy 31, 33, 88, 91
Tomb of Seti I 33, 87, 88, 110
Tombs of the Nobles 47, 89
transcendental reality 113
Triad 108
Trinity 10, 111
Turkey 25, 78, 81, 102
Tutankhamun 91
Tutankhamun, Pharaoh 91
Ubuntu 23
Uganda 15, 72, 102
Understanding 113
Unesco 66
United Nations 67
United States of America 17
Universal Consciousness 111
Upanishads 111
Upper Egypt 8, 9, 23
Ur 25, 75
USA, West 115

Vedanta 77
Vedic 84, 109
Virgil 24, 25, 102
Vishnu 69
Volney, Count 14, 102
Waddel, W. G. 62, 102
wars 4, 12, 75
Waset 10, 26, 85, 108
West Africa 15, 72, 101
West, John Anthony .. 64, 65, 66, 95, 102
Western civilization ... 12, 18, 23, 60
Western Culture 22, 23, 60
Western, West 15, 64, 65, 66, 72, 81, 101, 102
White 6, 69, 70, 102
Williams, Chancellor 66, 102
Wisdom 26, 110
Wisdom (also see Djehuti) 26
Wisdom (also see Djehuti, Aset) 26, 110
Witness 77
Wolof 101
Yellow 70
Yoga .. 4, 77, 108, 109, 110, 111, 112, 114, 115
Zaire 72
Zeus 24
Zoroastrian, Zoroastrianism ... 63

Other Books From C M Books

P.O.Box 570459
Miami, Florida, 33257
(305) 378-6253 Fax: (305) 378-6253

This book is part of a series on the study and practice of Ancient Egyptian Yoga and Mystical Spirituality based on the writings of Dr. Muata Abhaya Ashby. They are also part of the Egyptian Yoga Course provided by the Sema Institute of Yoga. Below you will find a listing of the other books in this series. For more information send for the Egyptian Yoga Book-Audio-Video Catalog or the Egyptian Yoga Course Catalog.

Now you can study the teachings of Egyptian and Indian Yoga wisdom and Spirituality with the Egyptian Yoga Mystical Spirituality Series. The Egyptian Yoga Series takes you through the Initiation process and lead you to understand the mysteries of the soul and the Divine and to attain the highest goal of life: ENLIGHTENMENT. The *Egyptian Yoga Series*, takes you on an in depth study of Ancient Egyptian mythology and their inner mystical meaning. Each Book is prepared for the serious student of the mystical sciences and provides a study of the teachings along with exercises, assignments and projects to make the teachings understood and effective in real life. The Series is part of the Egyptian Yoga course but may be purchased even if you are not taking the course. The series is ideal for study groups.

Prices subject to change.

1. EGYPTIAN YOGA: THE PHILOSOPHY OF ENLIGHTENMENT An original, fully illustrated work, including hieroglyphs, detailing the meaning of the Egyptian mysteries, tantric yoga, psycho-spiritual and physical exercises. Egyptian Yoga is a guide to the practice of the highest spiritual philosophy which leads to absolute freedom from human misery and to immortality. It is well known by scholars that Egyptian philosophy is the basis of Western and Middle Eastern religious philosophies such as *Christianity, Islam, Judaism,* the *Kabala*, and Greek philosophy, but what about Indian philosophy, Yoga and Taoism? What were the original teachings? How can they be practiced today? What is the source of pain and suffering in the world and what is the solution? Discover the deepest mysteries of the mind and universe within and outside of your self. 8.5" X 11" ISBN: 1-884564-01-1 Soft $19.95

2. EGYPTIAN YOGA: African Religion Volume 2- Theban Theology U.S. In this long awaited sequel to *Egyptian Yoga: The Philosophy of Enlightenment* you will take a fascinating and enlightening journey back in time and discover the teachings which constituted the epitome of Ancient Egyptian spiritual wisdom. What are the disciplines which lead to the fulfillment of all desires? Delve into the three states of consciousness (waking, dream and deep sleep) and the fourth state which transcends them all, Neberdjer, "The Absolute." These teachings of the city of Waset (Thebes) were the crowning achievement of the Sages of Ancient Egypt. They establish the standard mystical keys for understanding the profound mystical symbolism of the Triad of human consciousness. ISBN 1-884564-39-9 $23.95

3. THE KEMETIC DIET: GUIDE TO HEALTH, DIET AND FASTING Health issues have always been important to human beings since the beginning of time. The earliest records of history show that the art of healing was held in high esteem since the time of Ancient Egypt. In the early 20th century, medical doctors had almost attained the status of sainthood by the promotion of the idea that they alone were "scientists" while other healing modalities and traditional healers who did not follow the "scientific method' were nothing but superstitious, ignorant charlatans who at best would take the money of their clients and at worst kill them with the unscientific "snake oils" and "irrational theories". In the late 20th century, the failure of the modern medical establishment's ability to lead the general public to good health, promoted the move by many in society towards "alternative medicine". Alternative medicine disciplines are those healing modalities which do not adhere to the philosophy of allopathic medicine. Allopathic medicine is what medical doctors practice by an large. It is the theory that disease is caused by agencies outside the body such as bacteria, viruses or physical means which affect the body. These can therefore be treated by medicines and therapies The natural healing method began in the absence of extensive technologies with the idea that all the answers for health may be found in nature or rather, the deviation from nature. Therefore, the health of the body can be restored by correcting the aberration and thereby restoring balance.

This is the area that will be covered in this volume. Allopathic techniques have their place in the art of healing. However, we should not forget that the body is a grand achievement of the spirit and built into it is the capacity to maintain itself and heal itself. Ashby, Muata ISBN: 1-884564-49-6 $28.95

4. INITIATION INTO EGYPTIAN YOGA Shedy: Spiritual discipline or program, to go deeply into the mysteries, to study the mystery teachings and literature profoundly, to penetrate the mysteries. You will learn about the mysteries of initiation into the teachings and practice of Yoga and how to become an Initiate of the mystical sciences. This insightful manual is the first in a series which introduces you to the goals of daily spiritual and yoga practices: Meditation, Diet, Words of Power and the ancient wisdom teachings. 8.5" X 11" ISBN 1-884564-02-X   Soft Cover $24.95 U.S.

5. *THE AFRICAN ORIGINS OF CIVILIZATION, RELIGION AND YOGA SPIRITUALITY AND ETHICS PHILOSOPHY* HARD COVER EDITION Part 1, Part 2, Part 3 in one volume 683 Pages Hard Cover First Edition Three volumes in one. Over the past several years I have been asked to put together in one volume the most important evidences showing the correlations and common teachings between Kamitan (Ancient Egyptian) culture and religion and that of India. The questions of the history of Ancient Egypt, and the latest archeological evidences showing civilization and culture in Ancient Egypt and its spread to other countries, has intrigued many scholars as well as mystics over the years. Also, the possibility that Ancient Egyptian Priests and Priestesses migrated to Greece, India and other countries to carry on the traditions of the Ancient Egyptian Mysteries, has been speculated over the years as well. In chapter 1 of the book *Egyptian Yoga The Philosophy of Enlightenment,* 1995, I first introduced the deepest comparison between Ancient Egypt and India that had been brought forth up to that time. Now, in the year 2001 this new book, *THE AFRICAN ORIGINS OF CIVILIZATION, MYSTICAL RELIGION AND YOGA PHILOSOPHY,* more fully explores the motifs, symbols and philosophical correlations between Ancient Egyptian and Indian mysticism and clearly shows not only that Ancient Egypt and India were connected culturally but also spiritually. How does this knowledge help the spiritual aspirant? This discovery has great importance for the Yogis and mystics who follow the philosophy of Ancient Egypt and the mysticism of India. It means that India has a longer history and heritage than was previously understood. It shows that the mysteries of Ancient Egypt were essentially a yoga tradition which did not die but rather developed into the modern day systems of Yoga technology of India. It further shows that African culture developed Yoga Mysticism earlier than any other civilization in history. All of this expands our understanding of the unity of culture and the deep legacy of Yoga, which stretches into the distant past, beyond the Indus Valley civilization, the earliest known high culture in India as well as the Vedic tradition of Aryan culture. Therefore, Yoga culture and mysticism is the oldest known tradition of spiritual development and Indian mysticism is an extension of the Ancient Egyptian mysticism. By understanding the legacy which Ancient Egypt gave to India the mysticism of India is better understood and by comprehending the heritage of Indian Yoga, which is rooted in Ancient Egypt the Mysticism of Ancient Egypt is also better understood. This expanded understanding allows us to prove the underlying kinship of humanity, through the common symbols, motifs and philosophies which are not disparate and confusing teachings but in reality expressions of the same study of truth through metaphysics and mystical realization of Self. (HARD COVER) ISBN: 1-884564-50-X $45.00 U.S.   81/2" X 11"

6. AFRICAN ORIGINS BOOK 1 PART 1 African Origins of African Civilization, Religion, Yoga Mysticism and Ethics Philosophy-Soft Cover $24.95 ISBN: 1-884564-55-0

7. AFRICAN ORIGINS BOOK 2 PART 2 African Origins of Western Civilization, Religion and Philosophy (Soft) -Soft Cover $24.95 ISBN: 1-884564-56-9

8. EGYPT AND INDIA African Origins of Eastern Civilization, Religion, Yoga Mysticism and Philosophy-Soft Cover $29.95 (Soft) ISBN: 1-884564-57-7

9. THE MYSTERIES OF ISIS: **The Ancient Egyptian Philosophy of Self-Realization** - There are several paths to discover the Divine and the mysteries of the higher Self. This volume details the mystery teachings of the goddess Aset (Isis) from Ancient Egypt- the path of wisdom. It includes the teachings of her temple and the disciplines that are enjoined for the initiates of the temple of Aset as they were given in ancient times. Also, this book includes the teachings of the main myths of Aset that lead a human being to spiritual enlightenment and immortality. Through the study of ancient myth and the illumination of initiatic understanding the idea of God is expanded from the mythological comprehension to the

metaphysical. Then this metaphysical understanding is related to you, the student, so as to begin understanding your true divine nature. ISBN 1-884564-24-0 $22.99

10. EGYPTIAN PROVERBS: collection of —Ancient Egyptian Proverbs and Wisdom Teachings -How to live according to MAAT Philosophy. Beginning Meditation. All proverbs are indexed for easy searches. For the first time in one volume, ——Ancient Egyptian Proverbs, wisdom teachings and meditations, fully illustrated with hieroglyphic text and symbols. EGYPTIAN PROVERBS is a unique collection of knowledge and wisdom which you can put into practice today and transform your life. $14.95 U.S ISBN: 1-884564-00-3

11. GOD OF LOVE: THE PATH OF DIVINE LOVE The Process of Mystical Transformation and The Path of Divine Love   This Volume focuses on the ancient wisdom teachings of "Neter Merri" –the Ancient Egyptian philosophy of Divine Love and how to use them in a scientific process for self-transformation. Love is one of the most powerful human emotions. It is also the source of Divine feeling that unifies God and the individual human being. When love is fragmented and diminished by egoism the Divine connection is lost. The Ancient tradition of Neter Merri leads human beings back to their Divine connection, allowing them to discover their innate glorious self that is actually Divine and immortal. This volume will detail the process of transformation from ordinary consciousness to cosmic consciousness through the integrated practice of the teachings and the path of Devotional Love toward the Divine. 5.5"x 8.5" ISBN 1-884564-11-9 $22.95

12. INTRODUCTION TO MAAT PHILOSOPHY: Spiritual Enlightenment Through the Path of Virtue Known as Karma Yoga in India, the teachings of MAAT for living virtuously and with orderly wisdom are explained and the student is to begin practicing the precepts of Maat in daily life so as to promote the process of purification of the heart in preparation for the judgment of the soul. This judgment will be understood not as an event that will occur at the time of death but as an event that occurs continuously, at every moment in the life of the individual. The student will learn how to become allied with the forces of the Higher Self and to thereby begin cleansing the mind (heart) of impurities so as to attain a higher vision of reality. ISBN 1-884564-20-8 $22.99

13. MEDITATION The Ancient Egyptian Path to Enlightenment   Many people do not know about the rich history of meditation practice in Ancient Egypt. This volume outlines the theory of meditation and presents the Ancient Egyptian Hieroglyphic text which give instruction as to the nature of the mind and its three modes of expression. It also presents the texts which give instruction on the practice of meditation for spiritual Enlightenment and unity with the Divine. This volume allows the reader to begin practicing meditation by explaining, in easy to understand terms, the simplest form of meditation and working up to the most advanced form which was practiced in ancient times and which is still practiced by yogis around the world in modern times. ISBN 1-884564-27-7 $22.99

14. THE GLORIOUS LIGHT MEDITATION TECHNIQUE OF ANCIENT EGYPT New for the year 2000. This volume is based on the earliest known instruction in history given for the practice of formal meditation. Discovered by Dr. Muata Ashby, it is inscribed on the walls of the Tomb of Seti I in Thebes Egypt. This volume details the philosophy and practice of this unique system of meditation originated in Ancient Egypt and the earliest practice of meditation known in the world which occurred in the most advanced African Culture. ISBN: 1-884564-15-1 $16.95 (PB)

15. THE SERPENT POWER: The Ancient Egyptian Mystical Wisdom of the Inner Life Force.   This Volume specifically deals with the latent life Force energy of the universe and in the human body, its control and sublimation. How to develop the Life Force energy of the subtle body. This Volume will introduce the esoteric wisdom of the science of how virtuous living acts in a subtle and mysterious way to cleanse the latent psychic energy conduits and vortices of the spiritual body.   ISBN 1-884564-19-4 $22.95

16. EGYPTIAN YOGA *The Postures of The Gods and Goddesses* Discover the physical postures and exercises practiced thousands of years ago in Ancient Egypt which are today known as Yoga exercises. Discover the history of the postures and how they were transferred from Ancient Egypt in Africa to India through Buddhist Tantrism. Then practice the postures as you discover the mythic teaching that originally gave birth to the postures and was practiced by the Ancient Egyptian priests and priestesses. This work is based on the pictures and teachings from the Creation story of Ra, The Asarian Resurrection Myth and the

carvings and reliefs from various Temples in Ancient Egypt 8.5" X 11" ISBN 1-884564-10-0 Soft Cover $21.95   Exercise video $20

17. SACRED SEXUALITY: EGYPTIAN TANTRA YOGA: The Art of Sex Sublimation and Universal Consciousness This Volume will expand on the male and female principles within the human body and in the universe and further detail the sublimation of sexual energy into spiritual energy. The student will study the deities Min and Hathor, Asar and Aset, Geb and Nut and discover the mystical implications for a practical spiritual discipline. This Volume will also focus on the Tantric aspects of Ancient Egyptian and Indian mysticism, the purpose of sex and the mystical teachings of sexual sublimation which lead to self-knowledge and Enlightenment. 5.5"x 8.5" ISBN 1-884564-03-8 $24.95

18. AFRICAN RELIGION Volume 4: ASARIAN THEOLOGY: RESURRECTING OSIRIS The path of Mystical Awakening and the Keys to Immortality NEW REVISED AND EXPANDED EDITION! The Ancient Sages created stories based on human and superhuman beings whose struggles, aspirations, needs and desires ultimately lead them to discover their true Self. The myth of Aset, Asar and Heru is no exception in this area. While there is no one source where the entire story may be found, pieces of it are inscribed in various ancient Temples walls, tombs, steles and papyri. For the first time available, the complete myth of Asar, Aset and Heru has been compiled from original Ancient Egyptian, Greek and Coptic Texts. This epic myth has been richly illustrated with reliefs from the Temple of Heru at Edfu, the Temple of Aset at Philae, the Temple of Asar at Abydos, the Temple of Hathor at Denderah and various papyri, inscriptions and reliefs. Discover the myth which inspired the teachings of the *Shetaut Neter* (Egyptian Mystery System - Egyptian Yoga) and the Egyptian Book of Coming Forth By Day. Also, discover the three levels of Ancient Egyptian Religion, how to understand the mysteries of the Duat or Astral World and how to discover the abode of the Supreme in the Amenta, *The Other World* The ancient religion of Asar, Aset and Heru, if properly understood, contains all of the elements necessary to lead the sincere aspirant to attain immortality through inner self-discovery. This volume presents the entire myth and explores the main mystical themes and rituals associated with the myth for understating human existence, creation and the way to achieve spiritual emancipation - *Resurrection.* The Asarian myth is so powerful that it influenced and is still having an effect on the major world religions. Discover the origins and mystical meaning of the Christian Trinity, the Eucharist ritual and the ancient origin of the birthday of Jesus Christ. Soft Cover ISBN: 1-884564-27-5 $24.95

19. THE EGYPTIAN BOOK OF THE DEAD MYSTICISM OF THE PERT EM HERU " I Know myself, I know myself, I am One With God!–From the Pert Em Heru "The Ru Pert em Heru" or "Ancient Egyptian Book of The Dead," or "Book of Coming Forth By Day" as it is more popularly known, has fascinated the world since the successful translation of Ancient Egyptian hieroglyphic scripture over 150 years ago. The astonishing writings in it reveal that the Ancient Egyptians believed in life after death and in an ultimate destiny to discover the Divine. The elegance and aesthetic beauty of the hieroglyphic text itself has inspired many see it as an art form in and of itself. But is there more to it than that? Did the Ancient Egyptian wisdom contain more than just aphorisms and hopes of eternal life beyond death? In this volume Dr. Muata Ashby, the author of over 25 books on Ancient Egyptian Yoga Philosophy has produced a new translation of the original texts which uncovers a mystical teaching underlying the sayings and rituals instituted by the Ancient Egyptian Sages and Saints. "Once the philosophy of Ancient Egypt is understood as a mystical tradition instead of as a religion or primitive mythology, it reveals its secrets which if practiced today will lead anyone to discover the glory of spiritual self-discovery. The Pert em Heru is in every way comparable to the Indian Upanishads or the Tibetan Book of the Dead." $28.95   ISBN# 1-884564-28-3 Size: 8½" X 11

20. African Religion VOL. 1- ANUNIAN THEOLOGY THE MYSTERIES OF RA The Philosophy of Anu and The Mystical Teachings of The Ancient Egyptian Creation Myth Discover the mystical teachings contained in the Creation Myth and the gods and goddesses who brought creation and human beings into existence. The Creation myth of Anu is the source of Anunian Theology but also of the other main theological systems of Ancient Egypt that also influenced other world religions including Christianity, Hinduism and Buddhism. The Creation Myth holds the key to understanding the universe and for attaining spiritual Enlightenment. ISBN: 1-884564-38-0 $19.95

21. African Religion VOL 3: Memphite Theology: MYSTERIES OF MIND Mystical Psychology & Mental Health for Enlightenment and Immortality based on the Ancient Egyptian Philosophy of Menefer -Mysticism of Ptah, Egyptian Physics and Yoga Metaphysics and the Hidden properties of Matter.

This volume uncovers the mystical psychology of the Ancient Egyptian wisdom teachings centering on the philosophy of the Ancient Egyptian city of Menefer (Memphite Theology). How to understand the mind and how to control the senses and lead the mind to health, clarity and mystical self-discovery. This Volume will also go deeper into the philosophy of God as creation and will explore the concepts of modern science and how they correlate with ancient teachings. This Volume will lay the ground work for the understanding of the philosophy of universal consciousness and the initiatic/yogic insight into who or what is God? ISBN 1-884564-07-0 $22.95

22. AFRICAN RELIGION VOLUME 5: THE GODDESS AND THE EGYPTIAN MYSTERIESTHE PATH OF THE GODDESS THE GODDESS PATH The Secret Forms of the Goddess and the Rituals of Resurrection The Supreme Being may be worshipped as father or as mother. *Ushet Rekhat* or *Mother Worship*, is the spiritual process of worshipping the Divine in the form of the Divine Goddess. It celebrates the most important forms of the Goddess including *Nathor, Maat, Aset, Arat, Amentet and Hathor* and explores their mystical meaning as well as the rising of *Sirius,* the star of Aset (Aset) and the new birth of Hor (Heru). The end of the year is a time of reckoning, reflection and engendering a new or renewed positive movement toward attaining spiritual Enlightenment. The Mother Worship devotional meditation ritual, performed on five days during the month of December and on New Year's Eve, is based on the Ushet Rekhit. During the ceremony, the cosmic forces, symbolized by Sirius - and the constellation of Orion ---, are harnessed through the understanding and devotional attitude of the participant. This propitiation draws the light of wisdom and health to all those who share in the ritual, leading to prosperity and wisdom. $14.95 ISBN 1-884564-18-6

23. *THE MYSTICAL JOURNEY FROM JESUS TO CHRIST* Discover the ancient Egyptian origins of Christianity before the Catholic Church and learn the mystical teachings given by Jesus to assist all humanity in becoming Christlike. Discover the secret meaning of the Gospels that were discovered in Egypt. Also discover how and why so many Christian churches came into being. Discover that the Bible still holds the keys to mystical realization even though its original writings were changed by the church. Discover how to practice the original teachings of Christianity which leads to the Kingdom of Heaven. $24.95   ISBN# 1-884564-05-4 size: 8½" X 11"

24. THE STORY OF ASAR, ASET AND HERU: An Ancient Egyptian Legend (For Children)   Now for the first time, the most ancient myth of Ancient Egypt comes alive for children. Inspired by the books *The Asarian Resurrection: The Ancient Egyptian Bible* and *The Mystical Teachings of The Asarian Resurrection, The Story of Asar, Aset and Heru* is an easy to understand and thrilling tale which inspired the children of Ancient Egypt to aspire to greatness and righteousness. If you and your child have enjoyed stories like *The Lion King* and *Star Wars you will love The Story of Asar, Aset and Heru*. Also, if you know the story of Jesus and Krishna you will discover than Ancient Egypt had a similar myth and that this myth carries important spiritual teachings for living a fruitful and fulfilling life. This book may be used along with *The Parents Guide To The Asarian Resurrection Myth: How to Teach Yourself and Your Child the Principles of Universal Mystical Religion*. The guide provides some background to the Asarian Resurrection myth and it also gives insight into the mystical teachings contained in it which you may introduce to your child. It is designed for parents who wish to grow spiritually with their children and it serves as an introduction for those who would like to study the Asarian Resurrection Myth in depth and to practice its teachings. 8.5" X 11"   ISBN: 1-884564-31-3 $12.95

25. THE PARENTS GUIDE TO THE AUSARIAN RESURRECTION MYTH: How to Teach Yourself and Your Child the Principles of Universal Mystical Religion.   This insightful manual brings for the timeless wisdom of the ancient through the Ancient Egyptian myth of Asar, Aset and Heru and the mystical teachings contained in it for parents who want to guide their children to understand and practice the teachings of mystical spirituality. This manual may be used with the children's storybook *The Story of Asar, Aset and Heru* by Dr. Muata Abhaya Ashby.   ISBN: 1-884564-30-5 $16.95

26. HEALING THE CRIMINAL HEART. Introduction to Maat Philosophy, Yoga and Spiritual Redemption Through the Path of Virtue   Who is a criminal? Is there such a thing as a criminal heart? What is the source of evil and sinfulness and is there any way to rise above it? Is there redemption for those who have committed sins, even the worst crimes?   Ancient Egyptian mystical psychology holds important answers to these questions. Over ten thousand years ago mystical psychologists, the Sages of Ancient Egypt, studied and charted the human mind and spirit and laid out a path which will lead to spiritual redemption, prosperity and Enlightenment.   This introductory volume brings forth the teachings of the Asarian

Resurrection, the most important myth of Ancient Egypt, with relation to the faults of human existence: anger, hatred, greed, lust, animosity, discontent, ignorance, egoism jealousy, bitterness, and a myriad of psycho-spiritual ailments which keep a human being in a state of negativity and adversity   ISBN: 1-884564-17-8 $15.95

27. TEMPLE RITUAL OF THE ANCIENT EGYPTIAN MYSTERIES--THEATER & DRAMA OF THE ANCIENT EGYPTIAN MYSTERIES: Details the practice of the mysteries and ritual program of the temple and the philosophy an practice of the ritual of the mysteries, its purpose and execution. Featuring the Ancient Egyptian stage play-"The Enlightenment of Hathor' Based on an Ancient Egyptian Drama, The original Theater -Mysticism of the Temple of Hetheru 1-884564-14-3 $19.95   By Dr. Muata Ashby

28. GUIDE TO PRINT ON DEMAND: SELF-PUBLISH FOR PROFIT, SPIRITUAL FULFILLMENT AND SERVICE TO HUMANITY Everyone asks us how we produced so many books in such a short time. Here are the secrets to writing and producing books that uplift humanity and how to get them printed for a fraction of the regular cost. Anyone can become an author even if they have limited funds. All that is necessary is the willingness to learn how the printing and book business work and the desire to follow the special instructions given here for preparing your manuscript format. Then you take your work directly to the non-traditional companies who can produce your books for less than the traditional book printer can. ISBN: 1-884564-40-2 $16.95 U. S.

29. Egyptian Mysteries: Vol. 1, Shetaut Neter What are the Mysteries? For thousands of years the spiritual tradition of Ancient Egypt, S*hetaut Neter,* "The Egyptian Mysteries," "The Secret Teachings," have fascinated, tantalized and amazed the world. At one time exalted and recognized as the highest culture of the world, by Africans, Europeans, Asiatics, Hindus, Buddhists and other cultures of the ancient world, in time it was shunned by the emerging orthodox world religions. Its temples desecrated, its philosophy maligned, its tradition spurned, its philosophy dormant in the mystical *Medu Neter,* the mysterious hieroglyphic texts which hold the secret symbolic meaning that has scarcely been discerned up to now. What are the secrets of *Nehast* {spiritual awakening and emancipation, resurrection}. More than just a literal translation, this volume is for awakening to the secret code *Shetitu* of the teaching which was not deciphered by Egyptologists, nor could be understood by ordinary spiritualists. This book is a reinstatement of the original science made available for our times, to the reincarnated followers of Ancient Egyptian culture and the prospect of spiritual freedom to break the bonds of *Khemn,* "ignorance," and slavery to evil forces: *Såaa* . ISBN: 1-884564-41-0 $19.99

30. EGYPTIAN MYSTERIES VOL 2: Dictionary of Gods and Goddesses This book is about the mystery of neteru, the gods and goddesses of Ancient Egypt (Kamit, Kemet). Neteru means "Gods and Goddesses." But the Neterian teaching of Neteru represents more than the usual limited modern day concept of "divinities" or "spirits." The Neteru of Kamit are also metaphors, cosmic principles and vehicles for the enlightening teachings of Shetaut Neter (Ancient Egyptian-African Religion). Actually they are the elements for one of the most advanced systems of spirituality ever conceived in human history. Understanding the concept of neteru provides a firm basis for spiritual evolution and the pathway for viable culture, peace on earth and a healthy human society.   Why is it important to have gods and goddesses in our lives? In order for spiritual evolution to be possible, once a human being has accepted that there is existence after death and there is a transcendental being who exists beyond time and space knowledge, human beings need a connection to that which transcends the ordinary experience of human life in time and space and a means to understand the transcendental reality beyond the mundane reality. ISBN: 1-884564-23-2 $21.95

31. EGYPTIAN MYSTERIES VOL. 3 The Priests and Priestesses of Ancient Egypt This volume details the path of Neterian priesthood, the joys, challenges and rewards of advanced Neterian life, the teachings that allowed the priests and priestesses to manage the most long lived civilization in human history and how that path can be adopted today; for those who want to tread the path of the Clergy of Shetaut Neter. ISBN: 1-884564-53-4 $24.95

32. The War of Heru and Set: The Struggle of Good and Evil for Control of the World and The Human Soul This volume contains a novelized version of the Asarian Resurrection myth that is based on the actual scriptures presented in the Book Asarian Religion (old name –Resurrecting Osiris). This volume is prepared in the form of a screenplay and can be easily adapted to be used as a stage play. Spiritual seeking

is a mythic journey that has many emotional highs and lows, ecstasies and depressions, victories and frustrations. This is the War of Life that is played out in the myth as the struggle of Heru and Set and those are mythic characters that represent the human Higher and Lower self. How to understand the war and emerge victorious in the journey o life? The ultimate victory and fulfillment can be experienced, which is not changeable or lost in time. The purpose of myth is to convey the wisdom of life through the story of divinities who show the way to overcome the challenges and foibles of life. In this volume the feelings and emotions of the characters of the myth have been highlighted to show the deeply rich texture of the Ancient Egyptian myth. This myth contains deep spiritual teachings and insights into the nature of self, of God and the mysteries of life and the means to discover the true meaning of life and thereby achieve the true purpose of life. To become victorious in the battle of life means to become the King (or Queen) of Egypt.Have you seen movies like The Lion King, Hamlet, The Odyssey, or The Little Buddha? These have been some of the most popular movies in modern times. The Sema Institute of Yoga is dedicated to researching and presenting the wisdom and culture of ancient Africa. The Script is designed to be produced as a motion picture but may be addapted for the theater as well. $21.95   copyright 1998 By Dr. Muata Ashby ISBN 1-8840564-44-5

33. AFRICAN DIONYSUS: FROM EGYPT TO GREECE: The Kamitan Origins of Greek Culture and Religion ISBN: 1-884564-47-X FROM EGYPT TO GREECE This insightful manual is a reference to Ancient Egyptian mythology and philosophy and its correlation to what later became known as Greek and Rome mythology and philosophy. It outlines the basic tenets of the mythologies and shoes the ancient origins of Greek culture in Ancient Egypt. This volume also documents the origins of the Greek alphabet in Egypt as well as Greek religion, myth and philosophy of the gods and goddesses from Egypt from the myth of Atlantis and archaic period with the Minoans to the Classical period. This volume also acts as a resource for Colleges students who would like to set up fraternities and sororities based on the original Ancient Egyptian principles of Sheti and Maat philosophy. ISBN: 1-884564-47-X $22.95 U.S.

34. THE FORTY TWO PRECEPTS OF MAAT, THE PHILOSOPHY OF RIGHTEOUS ACTION AND THE ANCIENT EGYPTIAN WISDOM TEXTS <u>ADVANCED STUDIES</u> This manual is designed for use with the 1998 Maat Philosophy Class conducted by Dr. Muata Ashby. This is a detailed study of Maat Philosophy. It contains a compilation of the 42 laws or precepts of Maat and the corresponding principles which they represent along with the teachings of the ancient Egyptian Sages relating to each. Maat philosophy was the basis of Ancient Egyptian society and government as well as the heart of Ancient Egyptian myth and spirituality. Maat is at once a goddess, a cosmic force and a living social doctrine, which promotes social harmony and thereby paves the way for spiritual evolution in all levels of society. ISBN: 1-884564-48-8 $16.95 U.S.

35. THE SECRET LOTUS: *Poetry of Enlightenment*

Discover the mystical sentiment of the Kemetic teaching as expressed through the poetry of Sebai Muata Ashby. The teaching of spiritual awakening is uniquely experienced when the poetic sensibility is present. This first volume contains the poems written between 1996 and 2003. **1-884564--16 -X $16.99**

The Black African Ancient Egyptians
Order Form

Telephone orders: Call Toll Free: 1(305) 378-6253. Have your AMEX, Optima, Visa or MasterCard ready.
Fax orders: 1-(305) 378-6253   E-MAIL ADDRESS: Semayoga@aol.com
Postal Orders: Sema Institute of Yoga, P.O. Box 570459, Miami, Fl. 33257. USA.
Please send the following books and / or tapes.

ITEM
_____Cost $_____
_____Cost $_____
_____Cost $_____
_____Cost $_____
_____Cost $_____
                                        Total $_____

Name:_____

Physical Address:_____

City:_____ State:_____ Zip:_____

Sales tax: Please add 6.5% for books shipped to Florida addresses
_____Shipping: $6.50 for first book and .50¢ for each additional
_____Shipping: Outside US $5.00 for first book and $3.00 for each additional

_____Payment:_____
_____Check -Include Driver License #:
          _____

_____Credit card: _____ Visa, _____ MasterCard, _____ Optima,
_____ AMEX.

Card number:_____
Name on card:_____ Exp. date:_____/_____

Copyright 1995-2005 Dr. R. Muata Abhaya Ashby
Sema Institute of Yoga
P.O.Box 570459, Miami, Florida, 33257
(305) 378-6253 Fax: (305) 378-6253

www.ingramcontent.com/pod-product-compliance
Lightning Source LLC
Chambersburg PA
CBHW081117080526
44587CB00021B/3632